TABLE OF CONTENTS

	Introduction	3
Chapter 1	Philosopy and Objectives	9
Chapter 2	Your Needs – Your Plans	19
Chapter 3	Your Staff	31
Chapter 4	Assessing Your Product – Your Teams(s)	53
Chapter 5	Budget and How To Improve	63
Chapter 6	Staff Assistance – Use of Volunteers	71
Chapter 7	Make Each Night/Day A Special Event – YOU ARE THE PRODUCER	77
Chapter 8	Important Extras To Get You Over The Top – Special Ideas To Get More STUDENTS Out To Your Games	93
Chapter 9	Use of Direct Mail and Personal Contact – "Getting The Word Out"	121
Chapter 10	Filling Seats FIRST – Next Step Is SELLING SEATS – Including Pricing	143
Chapter 11	Motivation and Encouragement – Your Scoreboard	169
Chapter 12	Ideas From Others	183
Chapter 13	Analyze – Analyze – Analyze; And Then Adjust. Fine Tuning Your Work	219
Chapter 14	Future Ideas – Where Do We Get Them?	227
Chapter 15	Author's Wrap-Up... And "Some Added Thoughts For Your Coffee Break"	235

... and, If you don't promote/market, a terrible thing happens...nothing.

NOTES

INTRODUCTION

Why a need for a book like this? The high schools and colleges today face more obstacles than ever before as they try to fill/sell seats. Of course, selling seats is much better than just filling seats. However, the first step is to FILL them.

More today than ever before, people have so many options for their free time. Television with all its different sports packages and opportunities to see great match-ups, is just one part of the problem. You add to this the physical fitness craze, increased leisure time activities to the increase in outstanding marketing of all events, and you can see the picture. Very good marketing people who believe in their product, can make their product very appealing. Today's marketing methods are so far advanced and effective that the schools have had a difficult time keeping up with all of this. Unfortunately, the last few years has seen the bizarre and different attract more viewers/customers i.e. the popularity of pro wrestling and the XFL football (this lasted just one year with a reported combined loss near 70 million dollars).

> **However, the colleges and high schools have a lot to sell and SELL THEY MUST.**

However, the colleges and high schools have a lot to sell and SELL THEY MUST. All sorts of creative marketing is needed today to get more people into those seats. First and foremost, prices for school events are much less expensive, the participants are amateurs, and generally more disciplined and maybe more apt to be a role model for today's youth. Most schools don't have quite the size of arenas or stadiums and consequently less of a crowd to fight. The more intimate atmosphere can be more attractive. There has been a certain backlash to the gigantic salaries of today's pro athletes as well. Prices to attend pro games have skyrocketed — the Dallas Morning News of Tuesday, July 11, 2000, in an article by Richard Alm, the outstanding sports business writer for that paper, stated that "a family of four would spend $161.13 attending a baseball game at Pac Bell Park (San Francisco), up 45.8 per cent from what it cost at 3Com in 1999, according to calculations by

Team Marketing Report, a Chicago-based consultant to sports franchises." Probably in pro basketball, the figures would be higher.

One of the concerns, when writing a book like this is to determine what fits your particular situation the best. What we've tried to do is throw out a lot of ideas that will fit most all situations and possibly each and every revenue – producing sport. Everything can't be done at once, so a PLAN is necessary — a WRITTEN PLAN. You need to pick and choose what is a good fit and a potential "home run" for your school. If it can't be a home run, make it a double or a triple because time and some money will be involved.

This book should be utilized as a combination textbook and workbook, geared to schools and athletic programs that are going through the "empty seat" problems. If that pertains to you, you are in the majority.

Having attended many high school and college games in my career in coaching, I am deeply concerned about this decline in attendance as well as spectator interest.

This book will allow you to "yellow highlight" to your heart's content. The sports marketing field has really become popular and appears to be an "in" field. It's so full of excitement. With more people in attendance, not only more money will be coming in, but also, you've created a much more favorable home atmosphere, with more excitement and fans really getting "in to" the games. Success breeds success.

Everyone enjoys a crowd with enthusiasm that involves the team, the band, cheerleaders, mascot and a large group of excited students/fans. We are in the education business — as well as the entertainment business and we need a budget and funds to conduct these programs. In most cases, the budget is already stretched, and quite possibly the fund-raising activities are also stretched — and when we look at our events, we see more and more empty seats. I recently spoke with a group of high school coaches in Houston, Texas, and during my talk, I said "raise your hand if you would like to see more people in the stands" and everyone of the eighty-some basketball coaches in attendance shot up their hands.

With those empty seats, let's begin to look at various ways we can start to fill them. It won't happen all at once, be patient and roll up your sleeves and start planning. It will take time and also usually take some money. However, within this book, we'll suggest various ways to get the job done effectively with a very limited or no budget at all. Let's hope you have at least a small amount of money budgeted for your use. If not, then we'll go to "Plan B" — some type of fund-raising activity that will allow you to get started; otherwise you'll have to work with strictly trade-outs and volunteer help. There's nothing wrong with that but it does limit you. IF YOU NEED TO RAISE FUNDS, I will suggest my previous book entitled: "How to Earn Dollars For Your Team/Organization/Club, by DIRECT MAIL" (see form in back for details). This is a way to raise funds rather quickly and it is easily repeated year in and year out.

I love the challenge that faces sports marketing people — it's EXCITING. You can actually KEEP SCORE just like your teams. In your office or another appropriate location, you can erect your own MARKETING SCOREBOARD with last year's attendance figures for a first game, second game, etc. and then fill in with your own current season's results after each game. Now, anyone visiting your office, can see what you and your staff have accomplished ... hopefully it's much improved. Sometimes it's difficult to obtain the actual attendance numbers from a previous season but somewhere you can get them, post them, and use these comparisons as an INCENTIVE and MOTIVATOR and also an excellent PUBLIC RELATIONS DEVICE ... and then when you get the SELL-OUTS, you have started to arrive. That's the objective of course, then you have to start thinking about adding seats (nice problem).

"GOOD THINGS COMETH TO HE WHO WAITETH, IF HE WORKETH LIKE HECK WHILE HE WAITETH."

> **"GOOD THINGS COMETH TO HE WHO WAITETH, IF HE WORKETH LIKE HECK WHILE HE WAITETH."**

(All quotes in this book are of unknown origin to the author, UNLESS otherwise noted — I love these quotes and only those that I feel are meaningful and appropriate for the purpose of this book/chapter, are included.)

CHAPTER 1

PHILOSOPHY AND OBJECTIVES —

"Every Seat NOT Occupied and/or Not Sold, Means Dollars Wasted/Lost"

MAXIMIZE YOUR SCHOOL'S MARKETING POTENTIAL. That is your job. You are in sports marketing – or want to be – what an exciting field. OPPORTUNITIES abound. When you excel and PRODUCE, upward mobility in this field is quite readily attainable and usually "no two days are alike". The marketing of sports is expanding – nothing monotonous about it and NOW it's an "in" profession. The sports world is looking for young creative talent with people skills and enthusiasm plus a willingness to work — you might as well include being a self-starter — and you must want to work because you won't find many shortcuts, if any.

As you look around the country, more professional teams are popping up (minor league baseball, hockey, soccer and arena football appear to be increasing in fan support). You add to this the increased number of outstanding games in various sports on TV coupled with Direct TV, it gets tougher and tougher to increase fan support for high school and college teams. Plus there are only so many dollars out there to be spent – the entertainment dollar has been stretched.

We've already mentioned the problems that come with decreased attendance and interest. It starts an ugly downward spiral which is difficult to catch and turn around. Empty seats affect everyone including the players, coaches, news media, and the fans, and particularly cash flow.

This book will outline steps/ideas to get started on increasing your attendance and deriving more income. At the same time, you create more interest in your team(s). It's an entire package which includes more than one person. It doesn't have to COST a lot of money; we'll discuss what we need and how we get started. Most schools are NOT excited about putting a lot of money into marketing their athletic teams. We certainly need to be CREATIVE to finance our budget as well as build a staff.

The "student intern" program discussed later, should give you a staff at little or no cost which will help implement your program and ideas. It's best to start small — and do it right with a small number of people involved (plus a small number of sports) and have it well organized and planned — then gradually expand your program/staff as needed.

Your PHILOSOPHY is simply to build fan interest, attendance, and increase revenue — and do it within the framework and philosophy of your school. You'll be doing all of the above at the same time.

I really like the SCOREBOARD idea. It promotes you and your staff and gives a terrific VISUAL PICTURE of how well you are progressing. Remember, give credit and encouragement to your staff as well as guidance, hands on training, and continued motivation Your job is TO INCREASE ATTENDANCE — your main sources for this are:

(1) Season-ticket sales (full and mini season sales or "pick your own games" etc.)

(2) Single-ticket sales

(3) Student ticket sales/attendance

> **Your PHILOSOPHY is simply to build fan interest, attendance, and increase revenue — and do it within the framework and philosophy of your school.**

(4)   Increase any front-row (ocean-front property) seating, box seats or luxury type seating.

(5)   Produce individually sponsored games; special nights/days, etc. — you might want to have each night/day sponsored by a different business/corporation depending on your town/city's size. We'll discuss later about the price tag you put on these special events.

(6)   Concessions

(7)   Parking (if you charge or not)

(8)   Game programs — can be difficult to "make money" on these BUT IT CAN BE DONE (we'll discuss in later chapter)

The objective of your PLAN — is simply to not only FILL but to SELL SEATS and increase revenue the best way you possibly can. You hope to create excitement/fun along the way. It's best to sell as many season tickets as possible -they become your ticket sale base. They are a constant — rain or shine. YOUR OBSESSION, as the person in charge of marketing the event, IS TO SELL OUT — STANDING ROOM ONLY.

YOUR JOB: MAXIMIZE YOUR SCHOOL'S

MARKETING POTENTIAL

"DO YOU KNOW HOW TO GET CUSTOMERS? — ONE AT A TIME".

Similar to the NBA's slogan as the strike season ended several years ago — "ONE FAN AT A TIME".

Former UCLA's great basketball coach, John Wooden's famous saying comes to mind , "Be quick but don't hurry".

Customers must TRUST YOU — you build trust by keeping promises and through good people relationships you BUILD TRUST, one person at a time also.

Customers must TRUST YOU

AS AN IMPORTANT aside to the schools — you need to do everything with CLASS — bizarre is usually frowned upon and can get you in trouble. Your thinking should be, "when in doubt – don't" or seek your supervisor's approval. We also know that generally beer and liquor advertising/sponsors need to be cleared by a supervisor also. Your school may have special rules and regulations for advertisers — know them and adhere to them — not try to circumvent.

If brand new on the job, here are some considerations for you as you get started:

No. ONE: Quickly assess the situation — find out what sports are to be involved and how much time do you have before that first season of that sport begins.

No. TWO: Quickly talk to TRUSTED PEOPLE WHO KNOW THE SITUATION — find out more information and get input... CAREFULLY ANALYZE. Determine what specifically are the main problems. TAKE NOTES.

No. THREE: Get your PHILOSOPHY together in writing (you should have this already).

No. FOUR: DEVELOP YOUR BLUEPRINT — YOUR GAME PLAN OF ACTION: put it in writing for yourself and your staff for others to see. Long term and short term. You know the problems; work YOUR PLAN FOR SOLUTIONS. Your objectives will be short term (for the most part). They will include plans to improve single game and season ticket sales, attendance by students, the visibility of the team, coach, and players, as well as increasing fan interest.

No. FIVE: GET STARTED. It's not that simple but you don't have time to do anything but WORK TOWARD YOUR TARGET.

No. SIX: Develop Your Organization... your staff.

No. SEVEN: Develop a timetable; your PLANNING CALENDAR, and if you have a staff, complete their job description.

No. EIGHT: YOU'RE UNDER WAY — good luck — slow down every once in awhile to analyze and re-think and maybe "tweak" things slightly to get better results.

ENJOY — GO GET EM

NOTES

CHAPTER 2

YOUR NEEDS — YOUR PLAN

The title of one of Dan Kennedy's books is "The Ultimate Marketing Plan — FIND YOUR MOST PROFITABLE COMPETITIVE EDGE — TURN IT INTO A POWERFUL MARKETING MESSAGE, AND DELIVER IT TO THE RIGHT PROSPECTS." This is "right on" — I can't make a better statement about marketing plans than that.

BUT FIRST ESTABLISH WHAT YOUR NEEDS ARE. Are you supposed to market one sport, two, three? After this is established, which sport comes first because you've got to get started immediately. You know the sport(s), you have written your objectives and philosophy, now you know your needs. Look at this carefully and then begin immediately on YOUR PLAN OF ACTION; YOUR BLUEPRINT. In developing this, KNOW YOUR GEOGRAPHICAL BOUNDARIES. You could waste a lot of time and dollars by going so far away from your "base of operations" that you have diminishing returns on your time. You would have financial and time drain instead of FINANCIAL GAIN. Carefully TARGET YOUR AUDIENCE and don't miss one person or one opportunity to GAIN A FAN — preferably a PAYING FAN.

The old adage: "PLAN YOUR WORK — WORK YOUR PLAN" is a must for your motto. In the business world, business plans are imperative for success and necessary for raising CASH to finance your work. Ditto for sports marketing with SCHOOLS. You need to get the OK and BLESSING of the person in charge, whoever you report to. It's much easier to SELL to your immediate supervisor your plan/idea by having it written and covering all the bases of what, why, when, cost, and other necessary items. You end your plan with the PROJECTED RESULTS — more revenue, more interest and enthusiasm and fans/supporters. Number of pages for this is a question most asked? It's up to you to estimate what will be needed to SELL YOUR BOSS?

> **Carefully TARGET YOUR AUDIENCE and don't miss one person or one opportunity to GAIN A FAN — preferably a PAYING FAN.**

The BUSINESS PLAN is also quite valuable for you to review from time to time to keep you on track — it also becomes valuable as you bring in workers/employees/interns to assist you with the job you intend to do. This shows others how organized you are and that you are PLANNING FOR SUCCESS. Computer programs are available for helping you with the development of business plans; however, you may, in your situation, have to go it alone and develop your own system to fit your particular school.

HOW DETAILED SHOULD IT BE? As detailed as you need it to be to get the necessary approval, first, and then for use as a successful operation of your plan. This is an oversimplification of an answer but that's simply the way it is, plus time is of the essence. This will serve as a BLUEPRINT for the successful conduct/results of your business. YOUR BUSINESS PLAN MUST REFLECT REALISM AND CONFIDENCE — you've got to make it work.

NON-STOP MARKETING — THE ENERGIZER BUNNY. Creativity meets PASSION. When I think of passion, I immediately think of DICK VITALE and his PASSION for his devotion to COLLEGE BASKETBALL. It's not work for Dick — it's love of the game and what he does — he enjoys what he does. YOUR PLAN shows research, analysis and thinking to your superiors and to those working WITH you.

> **YOUR BUSINESS PLAN MUST REFLECT REALISM AND CONFIDENCE — you've got to make it work.**

> **NON-STOP MARKETING — THE ENERGIZER BUNNY.**

Immediately work to obtain a mailing list and to BUILD ON THAT LIST.

Who do you concentrate your selling on? Begin with the base you already have unless you're in a brand new school. Immediately work to obtain a mailing list and to BUILD ON THAT LIST. You have the names and addresses of all of the parents of those in school (remember your geographical boundaries). Get a first class mail letter (it can be several pages to be more effective) out to the existing season ticket holders and what ever list you have, and include schedules, upcoming events, etc. Ask them for names/addresses of those friends of theirs that you can write to – perhaps conduct a "Every Season Ticket Holder get a new Season Ticket Holder" campaign. Reward those that come through with friends who purchase, with two free tickets to the Spring Football Game, alumni soccer game or basketball exhibition game with preferred seating or parking – make it attractive. Get a committee together, and/or a booster club, and have them give you FIVE TO TEN names and addresses of "potentials".

Once you get the names/addresses of possible buyers of tickets, you have TO GET THEM TO ACT — RESPOND — PURCHASE. You need to have something to interest them — as a bonus to responding if you are doing this by direct mail. YOU MUST DEVELOP AN ATTRACTIVE SALES OFFER. Small low cost give-aways such as key chains are used as well as team posters, coasters, scratch pads, and the like.

YOU MUST DEVELOP AN ATTRACTIVE SALES OFFER.

Larger committees of 100 or 50 are valuable — particularly if each gets you ten "potentials" — however, the larger committees are more often used for fund raising for larger sums of money.

Placing your pocket schedules and ticket flyers on the counters of banks, supermarkets, gas stations, convenience stores, hotels, restaurants, fast food restaurants can get the message out inexpensively. In this way, you flood the geographical area. Another way to get the message out is with the flyer with a rubber band placed on the doorknob of homes. You could use volunteers to handle this but make sure they have an assigned number of streets and blocks so you don't have duplication.

Any time you are working with a group going out to help you market, it's always helpful to make it a fun time by having some refreshments before kicking off the distribution (perhaps with a small pep rally, cheerleaders plus instructions as well as letting them know how important they are to you.) Then find time to FOLLOW-UP with a letter of thanks to all who helped.

> **Then find time to FOLLOW-UP with a letter of thanks to all who helped.**

After all this, hopefully not too much time has elapsed, as You HAVE TO GET OUT — SHAKE HANDS — MEET AND GREET — individuals and corporations. You have your plan in place, hand out something to each — be sure you have YOUR PRINTED BUSINESS

> ... and remember the SEASON for sports marketing — IT'S TWELVE MONTHS OUT OF THE YEAR.

CARDS (plenty of them) and get the cards from those that you meet. You need to ask for support and you have to SELL the benefits and the strengths of your team(s) ... and remember the SEASON for sports marketing — IT'S TWELVE MONTHS OUT OF THE YEAR.

Throughout this book, we'll have ideas to get more STUDENTS INVOLVED with your teams — THIS IS MOST IMPORTANT. Students are the heart and soul of your games — enthusiastic, optimistic, a little crazy and always psyched for the game. We'll also discuss your own student cheering section and giving it a name — like the Zoo Crew, Cameron Crazies, Rambler Rowdies, Xavier Zanies, and your imagination comes up with more. You can always get your team's players to get the students out to games. They need their own section — close to the field/court and maybe near the band.

On your checklist — don't forget to do everything you possibly can to make your arena/field FAN FRIENDLY — and that includes security. We'll discuss more in detail the IMPORTANCE OF IMPROVING GAME MANAGEMENT.

Set up an organizational one-year PLANNING CALENDAR for your season(s). Constantly add and subtract, analyze — make sure you have dates in which to send out season ticket requests, reminders on when certain

> Students are the heart and soul of your games — enthusiastic, optimistic, a little crazy and always psyched for the game.

items go to the printer for schedules, posters, and whatever, for each of the sports involving you. Include information in advance, if you can, on your banquets, tip-off or kick-off breakfasts, luncheons or dinners and any and all get-togethers. TIME MANAGEMENT is a key for you as the "chief" of operations; then staff selection and management comes next and keeping your staff informed and motivated.

Weekly STAFF MEETINGS are in order for most of the year — a break every once in awhile is good. Refreshments and/or a season-ending breakfast or luncheon for your staff is a good idea. Remember, staff/board meetings should be a board meeting, not a meeting of the "bored". Having each area of your operation responsible for a weekly report in digest form keeps your staff better informed and "in the loop". It's YOUR responsibility to keep the meeting MOVING. You should not only designate a starting time but a PROJECTED ENDING TIME. It should be an INTERESTING and INFORMATIVE meeting. Take a brief minute or two to reflect and review AFTER the meeting. This is a good SELF-TEST on your effectiveness as a leader. Of course, have notes taken and typed promptly and sent to each attendee. You don't want OLD news sent out. From time to time you have to remind ALL that staff meetings are CONFIDENTIAL and all info kept within the meeting room only. If items are felt to be real significant, you can

> **Remember, staff/board meetings should be a board meeting, not a meeting of the "bored".**

> **staff meetings are CONFIDENTIAL**

have a press release of "progress" or "decisions", prepared by your media relations department. At your meetings, you should allow ALL in attendance an opportunity to bring up any creative ideas that will benefit the group. Those missing the meeting should be responsible for sending a replacement with a written update. Complete NOTES need to be kept and filed and available at each meeting in case of need for review.

If meetings are less frequent during the summer months or off-season, as they should be, delegate PROJECTS to be completed by each — and give a due date including copies for all. These should be worthwhile and meaningful projects that will benefit your aims and objectives.

Attendance at LOCAL SERVICE CLUBS can be most beneficial and educational for those attending. Make sure you have plenty of schedules/posters/ticket information that you can make available to each attendee. Volunteer to speak on one or more occasions so that you can further market and get your message across. It's also a great opportunity to have your coaches on the speaking schedule — as well as a great opportunity to NETWORK and exchange more business cards.

Another NETWORKING device is an outing for the news media and selected heavy hitters — golf or just a breakfast or luncheon — and have your coaches or the coach in season in attendance. Very popular too, is just taking your coach and the two of you stop by the local newspaper to chat.

"Those Who Say They CAN and those who say they can't are usually both right" — Henry Ford

"Identify the problem(s) before you try to solve it (them)".

SOMETHING IMPORTANT WE HAVE TO ADDRESS : Championship teams generally mean sold-out arenas/stadiums. "Build it and they will come" usually means new stadium/arena sell-outs. Losing teams equate to poor attendance. Actually, all three situations we just mentioned, aren't necessarily true. What happens with a losing team? Worse yet, what happens when you've got a team of UNDERACHIEVERS and that's not exciting. Now you've got a problem, and it might be a big one. Your job becomes more and more difficult.

Now, with the losing and uninspired play of a team, let's hope you had a great pre-season ticket sale. Season tickets and pre-season sales are the best hedge on a team having a losing season. Second is the fact you and your staff have to work harder and harder to promote special nights/days to come close to your single-game ticket sale projections. It becomes a big job to keep yourself highly motivated. The same applies to the coaching staff as well — you and your staff being upbeat and enthusiastic helps them. You also need

> "Those Who Say They CAN and those who say they can't are usually both right" — Henry Ford

to keep encouraging your staff to PICK IT UP A NOTCH and to be more enthusiastic and fan friendly than ever. We will have more rolling up the sleeves, more meetings, more creativity for sales, and more upbeat attitude — that's a lot of "more of's" but NECESSARY to keep sanity and the ship afloat. It's during these times that you really earn your salary and then some. You keep looking for the "light at the end of the tunnel" and by now, you're fairly sure that it's a freight train coming through. These are the "dog days" for everyone but you can't let your people answering the phone appear "down" and tired; and tired you get during these seasons. It's important that you all stick together — continue to work more and more as a team – an upbeat team.

You might surprise the team at practice with some cheerleaders, pep band, and the mascot to help project some confidence and support out there when you're losing. It gets lonely out there when you're losing. Your selling/filling seats GAME PLAN begins with:

1. Selling more season tickets
2. Getting more students to attend (either students free or having a minimal season ticket charge like $10.00 or $15.00 for the season DEPENDING ON YOUR AVAILABILITY OF SEATS AND

DEMAND. Making sure your students are SITTING BEHIND THE TEAM — this will add to the attractiveness of "being there" and also to the EXCITEMENT in your stadium/arena. Have your band nearby also — unless you want to place them near the opponent's bench (an old trick and one that generally the rules of the league probably prohibit).

3. Selling more single game tickets

4. Selling more corporate sponsorships for games/events and for your "naming rights".

5. Involving more "SPECIAL NIGHTS" like family night, boy/girl scout nights/days, etc.

6. When you package your season tickets into a smaller number than a full season ticket, try to get balance; top teams, lower division teams, Saturday, and any other factors that your schedule would bring should be considered. Remember that for some reason, either cost or too many nights out or some other excuse that they can't do the full package, they're paying up front and that's a bonus.

7. Utilize your LOGO extensively.

8. Utilize your mascot extensively.

NOTES

CHAPTER 3

YOUR STAFF

In our schools, we have a tremendous resource — our students. Couple that with, in sports marketing, we have a "hot" profession — let's think about combining the two.

But first, you may be able, with your budget, to HIRE several staff members to form your staff. First and foremost, is probably an administrative assistant, to handle all the office work and anything that you feel is necessary. He/she must be able to handle everything, basically, especially when you are out of the office "meeting and greeting". WRITE UP YOUR JOB

DESCRIPTIONS — and be specific. You'll list all the areas of competence this person needs to efficiently and effectively handle the job. As needed, you will need to hire more staff including help with accounting, media relations, sales, ticket office sales, etc This begins to become quite costly.

Your staff needs are going to be in direct proportion to the number of sports you will be marketing. What kind of money will be in your budget? Each school is different in so many aspects – including money available for marketing the teams; number of teams you are working with; number of paid staff; number of seats available; socio-economic background of the school district, size of school, size of alumni base, etc. My next person to HIRE after my administrative assistant, would be an ASSOCIATE who would be like yourself — a "do everything" person. .By the way, "titles" are important — ranking right behind salary and benefits.

We've mentioned the "hiring" of a staff if you have the money in your budget. Let's look at some other options available to you, particularly let's examine what possibilities are available to you if you don't have money in your budget to pay a staff. DO YOU HAVE A SPORTS MARKETING CLASS in your curriculum? If not, would it be possible to develop a brief on why this might be an important addition to your curriculum? If you do have it, is it a two semester course or one semester? I've often thought that in addition to a first semester class, students for that class should have to report early to help all get ready for the marketing of the upcoming football season. If you don't and can't have the marketing class, can you work with the head of the Business department to "work study" a program in sports marketing? You could work with them in the development of this special program. "Where there's a will, there's a way".

The last pages in this chapter begin with a very interesting article taken from the January 31,1994, issue of CRAIN"S CHICAGO BUSINESS. It's titled: "The Name of Kenosha's Game: Marketing Class Reaches Local Firms Through Sports". I filed this away as I had been thinking about writing this book. I was fortunate enough to get in touch with the current director of Sportainment at Bradford High School, Sara Balistrieri, and be also able to reach Jeff McCauley who started it. Both were very pleased to discuss their programs and both are most enthusiastic about their involvement with sports marketing. At the end of the chapter we have wonderful comments about their involvement and direction of their work. I really appreciated their taking the time to share their experience with us. Jeff has relocated to Layton, Utah, where he heads his PrepSportsBiz. THANKS much to Sara and Jeff.

Another possibility would be through the use of "student interns" — the popularity of the field coupled with the student's need for work experience, and your low budget, make this a viable option. You need to determine which students would be interested in this and who would excel. To help with background checks and references, you could visit with the head of the business department or dean of the business school. Your ideal situation would be to have a junior backing up a senior so you have a smooth continuity of experience . You would offer no pay; but you can offer work experience in a field they may eventually choose to go into. You can promise a good reference IF they do a good job for you; and that you can "HELP" them get a job, you can't necessarily "GET" them a job. You could develop an entire staff from this great employment source – your student body. BUT FIRST, HOLD ON — you have to be able to TEACH this staff (written job descriptions a MUST plus provide close supervision and the necessary motivation). You can't afford any kind of sloppy production, nor can you "assume" anything — you need SUPERVISION. They are "in training" but you can give them titles and you can create a positive work atmosphere. You are setting the tone for proper work habits and standards of excellence. YOU can set a great example to these important co-workers of yours . I've always hated the word, "Boss" — they are important co-workers in your administrative TEAM.

PROBLEMS to overcome: You'll need to investigate a <u>flexible work schedule</u> because these are full-time students you are working with You might be able to get one person for two hours in the morning or all morning and another to handle the afternoons and an "alternate" over lunch hour to handle the phones and basic correspondence or mail-outs. Two: You need WORK SPACE for your team. Again, a problem but perhaps you can work around this. Three: Can you get them some kind of academic credit for their work? This would certainly help and add to the possibilities of building a strong staff. The better the staff, the better the results. In your selection of staff process, you need people with enthusiasm, students who will "enjoy" what they are doing and sports marketing. The selection process is most important. You don't need "PRETENDERS." Your motto might be: "No one ever said it was going to be easy".

"No one ever said it was going to be easy".

NOW, let's look at the possibilities for the make-up of your STAFF.

1. You already have the all-important administrative assistant.
2. You may have your associate director of marketing in place. He/she would be directly in charge in your absence allowing you to get out and work.

3. The above may be students if you don't have the budget for a full-time staff; next could be an assistant sales coordinator — working mostly the correspondence/telephones, and follow-ups for the director.

4. A Media Relations person (student) — again you are getting recommendations from the business or English department. This person would be in charge of press releases, helping to "create good news" with your help, in charge of the newsletters, statistic crews and media appointments.

5. A computer whiz is always important as they could help set up the web site as well as producing computer art; printouts, schedules, and various flyers you would need — would work closely with the admin. assistant.

6. You could add a financial analyst who would be in charge of the accounting/ bookkeeping (you might have a faculty member directly over-see this VERY IMPORTANT ACTIVITITY as a checks and balances arrangement).

7. Now adding to your team depends on your immediate needs. Do you have the physical space for an office? Will this group be unwieldy? Will they fit into "YOUR TEAM"? Additions might be:

   a   Video and photo coordinator

   b. Art Director — help in producing creative flyers/posters.

   c. Assistant to the Media Relations person.

   d. Student Game Manager to assist your Game Manager.

   e. Game production manager (for various pre- and post-game activities as well as half-time, National Anthem, etc.)

Somewhere in your organization/team, you might want to add another unpaid consultant — an ATTORNEY. There's usually a lawyer around who's a big sports fan. This would be an important "on call" position. All the above would have a job description (written) along with specific title, duties, and responsibilities. You might want to add a Director of Student Sales/attendance for games to help get the students out to games. You must over-see this staff and direct.

Your STUDENT INTERNS, by the way, can all be involved in a SPECIAL PROJECT and that would be to help you develop a plan to get more students to the games. Students are the backbone for crowd noise and enthusiasm that coincide with the efforts of the cheerleaders, band and mascot. It's a great combination — one that you can build on until it becomes a tradition. The students on your marketing team will be able to come up with good ideas and they personally can spearhead the drive for better numbers. Any time-out and/or half-time contests involving the students become very popular events – and it gives them an opportunity to win something also. Students provide a lot of entertainment and enthusiasm and are quite creative with their cheering – some times, too much so, but that's another story.

A neat way to get students more interested is to take the coach to areas where students congregate. With the colleges, you can provide in-person visits with players and coaches to your student centers, or various locations where students either get together or hang out. When I was at Duke I used to make a yearly visit to the Law School over the lunch hour and always had a great time with these students. Also with the colleges, I did what they called "Firesides" at Northwestern University. We'd schedule in advance and sometimes I would do one fraternity or sorority at 7:00 p.m.

(immediately after our practice was over) and another at 8:30 p.m. I always took pocket schedules, ticket flyers and posters. It was a lot of fun to answer questions, give out basketball T-shirts, and mix with the students. I got to the point where my student intern booked me at the various spots and we'd jump in the car after practice and head to a "Fireside". We also did various "living groups". The student intern would have the schedules and posters all ready to go and off we'd go.

For high schools, your student interns can recommend the best locations for you and the coaches to visit with students. In these sessions, you have the opportunity to let the students know how important they are to the success of the team. Coaches and players love terrific student support and sincerely believe that they can help them win and create a terrific home team advantage. Wherever you go to visit with students, take along a good supply of schedules and posters. In your talks, create a fun atmosphere and take a few of your players along with you.

Remember, don't confuse activity with accomplishment. This is most important as some feel that pizzazz is more important —don't fall into what I call "the activity trap".

ANOTHER good vehicle for you is the NEWSLETTER — this is a great activity for a student. Each sport should have one as it gets out the good

Remember, don't confuse activity with accomplishment.

news, however, you must emphasize that it be current. You can work on improving that mailing list but by now it will be growing in size. One of the college basketball newsletters that I have enjoyed is the one that Davidson College produces. It's very interesting and informative and keeps you posted on a variety of subjects including what former players are doing today, a look at the upcoming schedule, and up-to-date statistics in all phases of the game including comments by the coach and updates on injured players. I had one newsletter from Connors State College in Warner, Oklahoma, that each issue would have a team picture of the team from previous years. It's always great to keep in touch with your alums and people enjoy the "What They're Doing Now" section.

One last thought on your student intern program. You might want to get an advisory board together to help strengthen and over-see your program. Perhaps various faculty could donate some time to assist you with various responsibilities that you supervise. Perhaps an English teacher can sort of over-see the media relations and/or offer suggestions regarding the press releases. The accounting teacher/professor could assist with the bookkeeping side of your team. as well as help with the auditing. COST CONTROL MUST BE A BIG CONSIDERATION — it's easier to spend money that it is to "make" money.

COST CONTROL MUST BE A BIG CONSIDERATION — it's easier to spend money that it is to "make" money.

Let your imagination, creativity and your "need" go to work — however, we caution again about trying to do too much too soon and spread yourself too thin.

It's an EXCITING THOUGHT that you can make such a big difference in game atmosphere with your marketing and promotions. It's a great opportunity to EXCEL ... and you should have FUN along the journey AND, don't forget the internet — the Websites — what a tremendous public relations vehicle that can be for you.

Once your staff is in place, your GOAL now is to create a smooth working team. A large part of this is developing a TRUST and confidence in each other.

YOUR TICKET OFFICE can "make" you or "break" you – service with a smile is a MUST – "the customer is always right" — effective and efficient — you are striving for all three of the above – this "team" must be a "team".

If needed, you could go with an all-student intern staff. You would name a "Student Marketing Director — you as one of the very few "paid" staff would have to exert tight control over this operation but it can easily be done. You would be involved in more closely monitoring everything and have a "hands on" approach to your job while exercising your leadership role

> **A large part of this is developing a TRUST and confidence in each other.**

It's being done in colleges and high schools and perhaps in a limited role, in junior high. This is introduction and experience in the great field of sports marketing – a glamour profession although there are some nights you're not so sure.

If you are utilizing an advisory board as volunteers, I would try to have one or two high tech people involved. They have great ideas, have the pulse of what's going and what's new. This might put you ahead of the game with updated ideas and input. In addition, a real computer guru would be a most welcome addition to any staff that I might set up.

"YOU MUST CREATE A SUCCESS ENVIRONMENT" … and maybe this is a good place to insert one of my favorite sayings/axioms: "IT"S NOT THE HOURS YOU PUT IN, AS MUCH AS WHAT YOU PUT IN THE HOURS".

There are several recommendations that I feel are very important to the "student intern program" if you so decide to implement. You will need careful SELECTION of your team members. I would require personal interviews with you as the sports marketing director. I would require four letters of recommendations; two coming from current teachers at your school and the other two coming from his/her home community (this may be college or high school). In your interview, I believe you need to carefully

> **"YOU MUST CREATE A SUCCESS ENVIRONMENT"**

> **"IT"S NOT THE HOURS YOU PUT IN, AS MUCH AS WHAT YOU PUT IN THE HOURS".**

explain the commitment needed and also the availability of time, the time of day would he/she be available and for how long? You should have your job description in hand, showing just what you need and want from this student. You need to determine how important it is to this person to be a part of your program and gain this valuable experience. Does he/she really have a sincere interest in the sports marketing field? These are questions you need to ask to determine the interest level of the student. There would be a real "time discipline" needed and this should be thoroughly discussed.

If in high school, particularly, I would send a letter home to his/her parents explaining your program and that their son/daughter is an applicant. I would include a copy of the job description and indicate the approximate time commitment needed. Also, I would explain in this letter the important benefits he/she would receive including your all-important recommendation for the resume' if the work, effort, and contribution was more than satisfactory. I would also explain that there is no compensation other than gaining very valuable work experience. I would also try to negotiate some kind of academic credit for this valuable contribution by the student. After all, we are preparing these young people for the future and, with the popularity and allure of sports marketing, this could be extremely valuable.

TAKEN FROM: CRAIN'S CHICAGO BUSINESS: January 31, 1994

The name of Kenosha's game: marketing

Class reaches local firms through sports

By NOAH LIBERMAN

These days, a corporation might pay $40 million to co-sponsor the 1994 Winter Olympic Games.

But in Kenosha, roughly $750 will secure title sponsorship of the Bradford vs. Tremper Alumni Series of high school basketball games between crosstown rivals.

For three years now, students in the "Sportainment" class at Mary D. Bradford High School have been marketing their school's athletic teams. To local companies—including retailers, restaurateurs and the cable franchisee—they offer game sponsorships, retail promotion opportunities and exposure on local media.

For local residents, they've made games into non-stop entertainment. Parachutists deliver the game ball, fans shoot baskets for $10,000 prizes and the crowd calls plays at football games—all events sponsored by Kenosha companies.

The class is the brainchild of teacher Jeff McCauley, whose curriculum combines classroom instruction with considerable practical experience. Students develop sponsorship proposals, pitch them to companies and coordinate the in-game events and retail elements that companies pay for. "There are other schools in the country that have a stronger classroom component, but I don't think there's any high school where the kids gain so much practical knowledge," Mr. McCauley says. In fact, the students carry business cards.

The program raised some concerns three years ago at its genesis, particularly over whether the class constitutes an excessive commercialization of amateur sports.

But Mr. McCauley says over time the program's educational value has become apparent: His students have received four-year college scholarships based on the marketing principles they've applied. Others have turned the education into work-study jobs with university athletic departments.

For the school, the game-time entertainment has boosted attendance by up to 400%, despite some lackluster teams. This puts revenue in the athletic department budget at a time when some schools nationwide are asking students to pay extra to join the basketball team.

But neither the students nor the school actually pockets sponsors' money. The sponsors' fee is channeled directly into entertainment acts or advertising for the event.

Bradford Principal Joe Mangi says the program addresses some broad financial concerns. "Teachers now understand that we need to market the things we're doing—we can't just remain in an ivory tower. We have to branch out and network...You can only sell so many candy bars and pizzas."

This is not to say the Sportainment students don't sell pizzas. This fall, DeRango's Pizza King restaurant sponsored "Pass & Run Night," at which 300 football fans received two-sided placards that read "Run" and "Pass." On selected downs, the fans voted for the type of play the Red Devil offense would run. (And sometimes, the coach paid attention.) In addition, DeRango's negotiated with students for that staple of sports sponsorships: the right to sell its product at the games.

The deals are structured this way to ensure a sponsor the valuable commodity of exposure—especially to a certain niche. "A lot of times we have trouble targeting a high school-age crowd," says Dave Barnes, owner of three Cost Cutters hair care franchises in Kenosha. "They don't spend a lot of time reading the paper, and for a small budget this is an effective way to reach that crowd." Cost Cutters pays $900 to reach students with a season-long slam-dunk contest at basketball games.

A Bradford basketball crowd last season was treated to the sight of a fan sinking a series of difficult shots en route to a payout in the Pepsi $10,000 Hoop Shoot. This happened just weeks before a Chicago-area resident grabbed national headlines with a $1-million shot at a Bulls game.

On the big night in Kenosha, the Sportainment students re-learned a valuable marketing lesson about exposure. Says Mr. McCauley: "We weren't swift enough to get the shot on videotape."

PrepSportsBiz

Email: reachme@PrepSportsBiz.com

Need Help? Go Back To School!

As collegiate and professional sports teams and leagues seek entry-level staff or interns they would do well to direct some of their efforts at the high school market. Since 1990, the number of high school sports marketing programs has increased steadily. Sports Marketing classes are, in most states, the fastest growing class offering in the area of marketing education.

As you would expect, the quality and array of experiences provided for students varies widely among high school programs. However, in many instances students are learning about the development of corporate partnerships, creating and selling sponsorships, and developing and implementing marketing plans. Perhaps of more importance to collegiate and professional marketing personnel, these students often gain valuable experience in game operations and event management.

What Are They Teaching At The High School Level?

There is no standard course outline or curriculum for sports marketing programs. PrepSportsBiz was founded with the goal of making life a little easier for high school sports marketing teachers by providing a suggested curriculum as well as the necessary teaching materials and resources. The industry-validated curriculum includes both the marketing <u>of</u> sports and marketing <u>through</u> sports.

The marketing <u>of</u> sports includes topics such as the Marketing Plan, Marketing Research, Event Management, Fan Fun Events, Licensing and Merchandising, Ticket Sales and Selling Sports on the Internet.

As far as marketing <u>through</u> sports, the following is covered: Definition and Uses of Sponsorship, Event Triangle, Sponsorship Growth, Why Companies Sponsor, How Companies Decide What to Sponsor, Pricing Sponsorships, Leveraging Sponsorships, Ambush Marketing, Measuring Sponsorship Results, Sponsorship Rights and Benefits, and Sponsorship Sales.

(A detailed suggested course outline is available by contacting us at <u>reachme@PrepSportsBiz.com</u>.)

In many programs students gain first-hand experience with developing, implementing and evaluating events. This process involves creative fan participation activities that are used during quarter or halftime breaks, booking professional entertainment acts, enhancing the event atmosphere with the effective use of music, gaining corporate support in the form of title and presenting sponsorships as well as advertising and promoting the events.

Those involved with the marketing and event management efforts of professional or collegiate teams should contact area high school marketing teachers. Sports marketing programs are relatively new and still offered at a limited number of high schools. However, there are over 3,000 high school marketing programs covering the fundamentals of marketing.

How Can We Utilize High School Students

Teams may make use of high school students in a variety of ways. Some schools offer work release programs that grant school credit for working in an area that reflects their career interest. There are obvious advantages to having a student support your team's efforts on a regular basis. In this instance, a student may be responsible for a specific aspect of marketing/promotion or may be in charge of a specific Olympic sport.

In other cases, students or classes may be available to work on specific projects. Imagine the benefits of having a group of 10, 20, or more students helping you administer a survey to develop a fan profile or help with the pre-game tailgate parties or fan attractions.

Professional and collegiate teams often struggle to capture the elusive teenage market. Why not create an advisory committee and seek input from members of this target audience? This is one more way of capitalizing on a resource that is virtually untapped.

From a personal perspective, I have had students from Sportainment (the sports marketing program I started at Bradford High School in Kenosha in 1990) receive scholarships to work for the athletic departments at several colleges/universities including the University of Utah, University of Tennessee, University of Wisconsin, University of Wisconsin-Parkside, and the University of Wisconsin-Green Bay. In addition, several students have interned with professional teams from the Arena Football League, Team Tennis, Minor League and Major League Baseball, and the National Basketball Association. In each case, the students were ahead of their peers because of their high school experiences.

The collegiate sports marketing directors enjoy a significant advantage by seeking out high school students. Typically, the student will attend the university and work in the athletic department throughout the four or five years necessary to get their degree. This has to be better than bringing in new interns every semester only to find out they're more interested in an autograph than in working and learning!

If you are with a collegiate or professional team and would be interested in finding qualified high school students, do not hesitate to contact PrepSportsBiz. We have a nationwide following and contacts in several states. We will do what we can to put you in touch with marketing or sports marketing teacher in your area.

Finally, PrepSportsBiz is always looking for sports marketing professionals willing to share their expertise with high school marketing teachers. If you have such an interest, contact us at reachme@PrepSportsBiz.com .

High School Athletic Directors

If you are a High School Athletic Director and have a marketing class or program in your school you have a distinct advantage. You should immediately get in touch with the marketing instructor. Check to see if there is any interest in working with the athletic department on marketing-related projects. Promise your support and encourage them to start a sports marketing class. However, a separate class is not a must. An interest in sports and working with the school teams is all that is necessary. Feel free to have them contact PrepSportsBiz for curriculum materials.

The Bottom Line

Our real message in this section is that there are literally thousands of high school students, with experience, that are looking for a chance to work with you. Those teams that recognize that a high school student is a viable resource of ideas and contributions will be the teams that make progress off the field.

If you would like a complimentary trial subscription to the PrepSportsBiz Weekly simply send us an e-mail with "Filling Seats=Dollars" in the subject line.

Jeff McCauley has taught Marketing for 20 years, and Sports Marketing since 1990. During this time he started Sportainment, the Sports Marketing program at Bradford High School in Kenosha, Wisconsin. The program was featured on ESPN and garnered attention from USA Today, Advertising Age and Fox News among others. Presented with the Innovation in Marketing Award from the Marketing Education Association, Sportainment has sent several students into the world of sports. McCauley has taught at both the secondary and post secondary levels and started PrepSportsBiz in 2000 to provide resources to high school Sports Marketing teachers. He is currently a high school teacher in Utah where he lives with his wife Cindy and their daughter Emily.

Congratulations, Bill on having the vision to write a book for the movers and shakers in sports marketing at the high school level!

At Bradford High School, in Kenosha, Wisconsin, we are proud to have one of the premiere sport and entertainment marketing programs in the midwest, if the not the country. People know us as *Sportainment*. Students come out of this program with internship offers from the "big leagues" and go on to study sports marketing in college while they work with the athletic programs to "beef up" their marketing efforts.

It is amazing to know that juniors and seniors in high school are getting more hands-on experience than most college students in the same area. Students return year after year and are excited that they have the ability to work with top people and top companies in the field of sport and entertainment marketing.

Now, you've heard sports...and nothing about entertainment. That is our focus in Sportainment. The program was built around the idea that even if our school's athletic teams are mediocre, the ability to retain fan involvement can happen. Our marketing and promotion efforts are full throttle during the football season and the men's and women's basketball season. Therefore, the Sportainment course is run for one semester during the first semester of the school year.

During the summer months, we spend time planning for the upcoming seasons. Our summer sessions include brainstorming themes for homecoming and, of course, our cross-town rival game! We also start to think about the idea of "events." It was once said, "It's not just a game anymore." That's exactly how we view the home football and home basketball games. The goal we set for ourselves is to make an event out of every match-up during the season. This is where the excitement begins!

The great events we host have included: K-Town Tip-Off (our version of a collegiate Midnight Madness), Holiday Hoopla (a holiday four-team classic), Myron Noodleman Night (a "nerdy" comedian), and Mascot Madness (an invitation of local mascots to be part of our evening at the arena). In addition to those "big" events, we also like to retain fan interest by building in "fan fun events." Things like, t-shirt tosses, $5,000 field goal attempt, $10,000 basketball shot, and great fun-filled ideas that require a lot of stuffing food into someone's fact! We have a blast and so do the fans. In some cases, what we do, makes the game.

Sportainment
Sport & Entertainment Marketing
3700 Washington Road
Kenosha, Wisconsin 53144
Tel/Fax 262.653.6128

A Division of Bradford Marketing Group

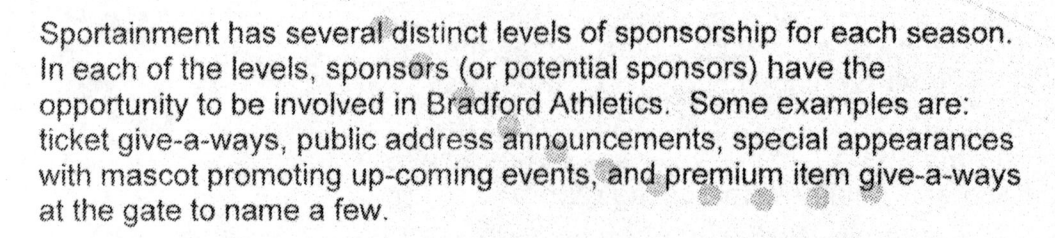

Sportainment has several distinct levels of sponsorship for each season. In each of the levels, sponsors (or potential sponsors) have the opportunity to be involved in Bradford Athletics. Some examples are: ticket give-a-ways, public address announcements, special appearances with mascot promoting up-coming events, and premium item give-a-ways at the gate to name a few.

Additionally, there is a formula that works for us when writing sponsorships. We have found that it has been instrumental to our success in selling sponsorship proposals.

I. Introduction...who we are and what we do—give them a reason to keep on reading.

II. Benefits...what will THEY get out of the partnership.

III. Target...the reach and frequency.

IV. Partners...who are other sponsors and why have you targeted them? What is the correlation?

V. Value...what is the total value of the sponsorship?

VI. Specific Considerations...anything that is not spelled out in the agreement that should be mentioned.

Without the basic formula for a successful program, like the ideas you have just read, we would not be where we are today. People at school and in the community recognize Sportainment for providing a fantastic learning environment for students and for brining the community a little closer together.

Our sincere THANKS to Sara Balistrieri who conducts this program at Bradford High School.

Sportainment
Sport & Entertainment Marketing
3700 Washington Road
Kenosha, Wisconsin 53144

Tel/Fax 262.653.6128

A Division of Bradford Marketing Group

Chapter 4

Assessing Your Product--

Your Team(s)

You have the responsibility of marketing several teams – you are trying to MAXIMIZE YOUR SCHOOL'S MARKETING POTENTIAL. I believe the COACHES and their staffs, including players, should play a prominent role in the promotion/marketing of your product. It makes sense because they are all the main players in your marketing endeavor. All of these people should be your best advertisement – they can get the "word out" to lots of friends, families, neighbors and the like, by their positive attitude and optimism. Their being "UPBEAT" and optimistic helps everybody and this image/projection is nothing but a BIG HELP to you.

The coaches and players have higher visibility and generally command more attention. If there is a radio, TV show, or website involved, the coach has a great opportunity to help your marketing through his comments and involvement. With entire coaching staff involvement, and particularly with the large numbers in football, and also in basketball, you can have a lot of "voices" out there to get a strong message to fans.

Scheduling the coaching staff for speaking engagements and personal appearances (malls are usually a good place to appear as scheduled) at local service clubs or other organizations is a must. It's best to have a meeting with the coaching staff so all of you are on the same page as to your sales pitch. You might even "script" some of the points of emphasis that will be shared with these organizations. All should be "armed" with a car full of pocket schedules, season ticket flyers, posters, and press guides. Press guides are more expensive to print, but these can be used as door prizes or handed out to only a select few. Again, try to get as many names and mailing addresses of all you meet and greet – ditto for business cards.

When it comes time to carefully select a "theme" for the upcoming season, it's important that you tie this in with style of play, exciting play, or a "gimmick type" nickname for the season. Style of play has really come into focus in the last few years, in the hiring of coaches. Some of the recent "hires" were coaches who utilize an exciting style of play – one that will attract more interest and more fans. In football, the spread the field, throw on every down, high scoring type of play has become popular – it's exciting and more points go on the board and you've got more to sell. In basketball, the running and pressing attracts — although WINNING brings more people out. But in the meantime, if you play an exciting style, and are aggressive, and really hustling — that can "bide" the coach and the marketing people some important time. Also, exciting players and those with record-breaking performances and/or big number players, will draw fans. Some coaches are reluctant to "sell" individual players because the "team" aspect is so important and they don't want to disturb this. Because of this, you'll probably have to "hype" the team.

Selling your facilities can be an important part of your marketing. In baseball, look at what the Cubs and Wrigley Field have accomplished. The same for Cameron Indoor Stadium for Duke University basketball. In basketball, the NBA has been so concerned about the lower scoring averages of teams that they have had many meetings to try to seek a solution to this so-called problem. But selling your facilities could be a "plus" for you if it has some identifiable features. The advent of stadium and/or arena corporate box seatings, convenience of location, chairbacks, and the suites, have allowed an increase in ticket prices. How about that front row at the Los Angeles Lakers games? It's a "who's who" and I've recently read that their seats for courtside (celebrity row) with Jack Nicholson, Dyan Cannon and company, are being raised to $1,350 per game (yes, per game). That's still $150 short of the New York Knicks front row (with Spike Lee and others). You can see the direction it's going. However, you with the school can make your pricing attractive to individuals, families, and corporations.

As you can see from the style of play and other factors, we are in the "entertainment" business as well as the "education" business. An enthusiastic and optimistic head coach and coaching staff can help you sell tickets and not only fill seats but also to sell seats.

Again, assess your product(s) and develop your game plan based on this. Any way you can tie in some "tricky" saying or motto for the upcoming year will help you sell tickets.

Everyone is looking at how they can increase their revenue so that it will be put right back into improving a certain sport or two – or the entire program. It's a vicious cycle — spend more to increase the budget so the coach has a "level playing field". If not, the coach may look elsewhere at an attractive offer that includes a larger salary, increased budget, and perhaps, a better chance to win more games. The latter is the "measuring stick" for a coach, along with an improved salary.

"Make the Big Time Where You Are" by Frosty Westering is a wonderful book to read. I love the title also. Frosty is the head football coach and professor of physical education at Pacific Lutheran University, in Tacoma, Washington. There was a quote attributed to Arnold Palmer at one time, many years ago, that basically said there were no major or minor sports. It's how you "approach" your sport – whether as a player or as a coach. You make it the big time where you are and whatever the sport. I would recommend that book to you.

> "Make the Big Time Where You Are"

You need a TEAM EFFORT to make your product the very best. There are so many people that are an important part of that TEAM — and YOU ARE THE LEADER. Those empty seats are staring you in the face with dollar signs on each of them – and NOW you've got a game plan to get fans in them. In making your product "BIG TIME" — you create an atmosphere that is conducive to winning, entertaining, and exciting. You've made the atmosphere "fan friendly" and you continue to strive to make it easier and more convenient for people to attend your games. You've got organized cheering, and coordination between the band and the cheerleaders

> You need a TEAM EFFORT to make your product the very best.

> ... you continue to strive to make it easier and more convenient for people to attend your games.

you've got a lively mascot in action.

and you've got a lively mascot in action. You should be working practically year round to get a rolodex file of entertaining half time shows — of course, in football the bands make it a great half-time. In basketball, you have all those time-outs and you can utilize this time to entertain in many different ways. Keep a set of 3x5 cards on your rolodex of ideas that you have seen at other games and/or hear about through your "networking" with your associates at other schools/events.

Make your entire product BIG TIME.

Make your entire product BIG TIME. You've got to continue to coordinate your various groups such as ticket personnel, ushers, parking and concession personnel, as well as security. Conduct dry runs to make sure your incoming traffic flows as smoothly as possible and same for those leaving the event. I have been to some games where a good job was done on the entrance but those leaving were left to fight for themselves. People caught in traffic jams coming into an event or leaving don't look forward to returning.

Back in the late seventies, when I was coaching basketball at Duke University, I went with our football team to play at the University of Michigan. I was curious to see what it was like to sit in the top or last row of a 102,000-seat stadium for one thing – and also curious to see how efficient they were with getting traffic in and out. The Wolverines did a good job on both counts and also on the football field.

Don't underestimate the IMPORTANCE OF GAME MANAGEMENT. The management of the game includes everything remotely involved with the game. It involves someone in charge getting everything working smoothly with clock-like precision. Even though you are not directly responsible for this, in most situations, you must work closely together with the game manager because it directly affects marketing your product.

Equipment functioning correctly, including the game clock and scoreboard, is an important area of responsibility for the game manager. Do you have substitute equipment and/or new game clocks/scoreboard and what is your emergency plan for everything? Also, how long will it take? If, in basketball, you have a broken rim or backboard, how long will it take for it to be repaired and the game can resume?

For game managers, the beginning of the season exhibition game is a terrific opportunity for a "dry run" for all involved in that game. The exhibition games are important, but they don't have the importance of a regular-season game. It's a great time to have a meeting of EVERYONE concerned with the management of the game PRIOR to that exhibition game. This includes the ushers, police, ticket people, at least one representative from the coaching staff of that particular sport, band and

> **Don't underestimate the IMPORTANCE OF GAME MANAGEMENT.**

> **It's a great time to have a meeting of EVERYONE concerned with the management of the game PRIOR to that exhibition game.**

cheerleader representatives, mascot, maintenance and repair people and parking personnel – ALL INVOLVED – for this pre-season meeting. Remember, you have this great opportunity with an exhibition/spring game prior to your actual scheduled games begin. EVERY POSSIBLE GROUP should have their person in charge at this meeting. It should be a COMBINATION PEP RALLY, MOTIVATIONAL, ORGANIZATIONAL AND PLANNING REMINDER AND RULES REVIEW all wrapped in to one. It's also a great time to let everyone know how important each are to the success of the season. Then FOLLOW-UP with a meeting two or three days after the event to DISCUSS WHAT IMPROVEMENTS CAN BE MADE to make everything work more smoothly for that next game. It's also important to have several student representatives in the meeting to discuss how important they are and also some guidelines for their involvement. If you are "selling" family entertainment, it's important that groups don't go in the opposite direction and offend the very people that are your "paying" crowd. This is a delicate situation to say the least.

If you have a local radio and/or TV station, work to get your games involved — if not for a season, for one or two games. If not, make sure you provide these people with easy access and your media relations people work overtime to insure their being taken care of. One of my favorite sayings is applicable here: "Good things cometh to he who waiteth IF he worketh like heck while he waiteth" — it takes WORK but it's exciting work and very little "dull time" in sports marketing.

> "Good things cometh to he who waiteth IF he worketh like heck while he waiteth"

NOTES

CHAPTER 5

BUDGET... and HOW TO IMPROVE

Decisions – Decisions – Decisions. Perhaps this chapter should be number two in the book. You've already identified what sports you'll be marketing. You've got your "game plan" and "blueprint for success" in place. Plus you have begun to get your staff in order. Now you have to allocate the various monies to the right spots so you can get the "most bang for the buck". You also have to find ways to increase attendance and at the same time, locate or raise additional revenue – to keep your program going forward. Your budget will determine the extent *to* which you can market your teams. You can do so much with "trade-outs" and volunteer help. However, IF this is what you have to start with, you get started immediately and then work to make improvements. Many times, this is the ONLY WAY to get started so make the best with what you have. Hopefully you have some money in your budget to get you started." Then it's up to you to obtain monies from as many different sources that will work for you — including early season ticket sales, fund raisers, booster club dues, donations, or whatever fits your situation.

I feel that a meeting with each head coach of the sports that you are responsible for marketing is necessary – he/she has to be aware of your budget restrictions and well as his/hers. You both probably share a tight budget. At this time you can determine from the coach exactly what he/she needs immediately in order to improve. The coach should put these immediate needs to improve the program, in writing, determine the approximate total cost, and any ideas that he/she might have on how to pay for it. This should be a priority in your pre-season discussions with the coach. I also believe that a similar meeting at the conclusion of the season would be worthwhile.

Ticket prices are covered in another chapter, however, it plays a very important part because of your budgeting of the income from this source. I believe that today, more than ever, a team has to be extremely cognizant of the make-up of teams on your playing schedule. Will you be playing rivals at home which can boost attendance? Will you be playing opponents on the road that require lots of money for transportation/travel? Is your league schedule such that you have an equal number of good drawing teams at home balanced with an equal amount on the road (then, of course, the next year you would be balanced also)? Your schedule becomes very important for many reasons. First, you need to win, and second, you need to be playing teams that fans are interested in coming to see play. You should really work closely with whomever is in charge of scheduling – they have to be reminded that you need to have good crowds — they want good crowds as well as the fans – so you have to schedule accordingly. It's time consuming but time well spent in trying to arrange it so you and your team have the advantage. You should check on other "draws" such as a nearby school that has a record-setting player or a team with national recognition — both factors help with getting a crowd. You can BUILD YOUR TRADITION through year in and year out smart scheduling. So you should develop with your coach, a PLAN for wins, marketing success, and reduced travel costs.

> **You can BUILD YOUR TRADITION through year in and year out smart scheduling.**

There are books and books on fund raising. There are a thousand different directions you can go to raise funds. But with your arena/stadium, you have some terrific opportunities. One very popular way is through corporate "naming" rights. Whatever you have "nailed down" might be a possibility for some one/or company to put their name on it. You can have locker rooms named after donors; bricks along the entrance with the names of donors on each; classrooms can be "sold" with a plaque on the door indicating the donor; you can "sell" individual games to corporate sponsors; you can add a new row of front row seats that sell at a premium price (all of these with money coming in up front), or whatever your creative mind develops. Of course, each school possesses different possibilities. The booster club with its newsletter and website is a good way to immediately bring in dollars. Just taking a long, hard look at your facilities will probably give you an opportunity to "put a price tag" on some of your "potentials".

I mention above about the possibility of adding more front row seats. The University of Houston sold out their new front row seats in basketball several years ago at $750 per seat for the season. When Clyde Drexler became the coach and it was a popular decision, they added another (2nd) row and raised the price to $1,000 per seat. They also did a neat bit of marketing by building a type of luxury box seating (alums helped with the building of same) and they were not real elaborate, BUT the three-year commitment came to $15,000 per box, three-years at $45,000 per box. An excellent way to add revenue to your existing facility. Many are doing this in football and basketball. SMU in basketball added the same last year. I can't believe how many opportunities are available to you to raise money. So many companies are into it that you've got a good chance to pick and choose. Many of your catalog companies handle merchandise and premiums and anything you want to sell. Even KRISPY KREME DOUGHNUTS has a flyer available entitled "FUND RAISING". It advertises, make up to 50% profit" and by the way, that's got to be an easy sell. Who would turn down buying Krispy Kreme doughnuts? However, individuals and corporations are not handing out money today like they used to a very few years ago.

Your planning and organization MUST include accurate record keeping. It must have a set of checks and balances for any expenditure — most require duplicate signing of checks. There are too many horror stories out there where problems started with sloppy record keeping. If you are utilizing the "student intern" staff, you need to have yourself and one other adult involved with signing off on all expenditures. Someone from the business department would be particularly valuable for this responsibility.

> **Your planning and organization MUST include accurate record keeping.**

One area of a budget where slip-ups might occur, happens in the area of "cleaning up" expenses after your games/events. You must allocate a certain number of dollars for this. Many schools have various other sports and clubs handle this as their own fund-raiser. It can save you money and can earn money for that group. However, it must be supervised and they have to be held accountable for doing a good job — otherwise you're wasting money.

Some of your costs can be reduced by "co-op" arrangements. With the printing of your tickets, an advertiser can come on board and share or take over the entire costs of the ticket by simply printing their advertisement on one side. In other areas such as posters, pocket schedules, media guides, event programs and parking passes, you can possibly "trade-out" the entire cost by allowing them prominent advertising space. Being creative to offset your costs is a part of your job.

> **A very important aspect of your responsibility is to "CONTROL COSTS". It's easy to spend money.**

A very important aspect of your responsibility is to "CONTROL COSTS". It's easy to spend money. There are many considerations in this area also. One very key option is to do as much of your work "in house" as possible. This includes utilizing your computer people to print your brochures and flyers, and most any printing and art work that you need done.

Use of advertising agencies and art work/graphics by professionals can be very advantageous — but expensive. Careful consideration must be made on the value you will receive for what you spend. Trade-outs for tickets are one option or you might have a pro bono opportunity with an alumnus or good friend.

> **Be realistic in everything you project. It's nice to aim high and be optimistic but it's better to be REALISTIC in your projections for income and expenses.**

Be realistic in everything you project. It's nice to aim high and be optimistic but it's better to be REALISTIC in your projections for income and expenses. Your job is a big one to try and hit that mark without over-estimating or under-estimating. This is one of the more difficult tasks that you'll have.

Build a trusted and reliable group of suppliers. You need people that are aware of your tight budget restrictions and will help you out with lower cost possibilities. Establish a great relationship with your suppliers/vendors, check out all opportunities for discounts and delayed payments – however, the latter must be agreed upon in advance or you'll have accounting problems. You want to investigate the possibilities of your suppliers advertising with you.

If you are not doing in-house printing (which you should because of lower costs), you should have a great relationship with a printer. You don't need delays for any reason — most of us need things from the printer "yesterday" — and a gentle reminder on the all-important proof-reading with double-checking and cross-checking. Always "proofread for thought/content; not just for spelling".

In your budget, don't forget to include money for your MASCOT and for probably at least two sets of uniforms and the cleaning costs that go with it. Include travel costs and meals. You'll want to include the MASCOT for a lot of events and for public relations. You'll particularly want the mascot

> **You'll want to include the MASCOT for a lot of events and for public relations.**

Make A SELL-OUT an obsession

for any events where kids are involved. Kids usually love mascots and if you have a really good personable, fun-loving mascot, the kids will follow him/her all over the place. Involve kids and the mascot at sometime during a game if its possible. I saw the Houston Comets (WNBF) mascot do a terrific job with kids during a game this past season. Any time you Have functions like banquets and booster functions or events in a mall, involve your mascot.

Make A SELL-OUT an obsession

CHAPTER 6

STAFF ASSISTANCE — Use of Volunteers

In your staff "flow chart," you can make good use of a group of people who just want to help. How many times have you heard, "if you need any help, give me a call"? How many times have we forgotten completely about this comment? Don't lose sight of these usually well-meaning people.

When you start this job, keep a file of those that mention this to you. The more you get out and about, the more you'll hear this comment. Make sure you get them first on your mailing list. Obtain their telephone numbers (both work and home), mailing address, e-mail address, and start to compile your list. They probably have to be gently reminded that this is not a "paying" job – unless you come up with some sort of a trade-out like tickets but usually you don't have to do this. ANYHOW, keep an ACTIVE FILE on these people. Get their business card if they have one. INCLUDE them on a mailing list that initially includes a brief THANK YOU to acknowledge their "sincere" interest. If you are speaking to any service group, you should bring this subject up and get those important names and addresses after the meeting. They can all add up. You build your mailing list like you do your customers – ONE AT A TIME, ditto with volunteers.

> **You build your mailing list like you do your customers – ONE AT A TIME, ditto with volunteers.**

Now, how and where do you effectively utilize this free help? You must have a worthwhile project or event that requires a large number of mail-outs. You'll now really find out who is sincere or who will be "out of town" that evening.

Phone-A-Thons can be an event that volunteer help could be used. After a brief orientation (be specific what is needed and how it's to be done), you can turn them loose on the phone to season ticket holders or potential customers. Be specific with your orientation part of your meeting and also make sure you emphasize how important they are to the success of your program. I remember at Duke University in my first and second years there, having a phone-a-thon for three straight evenings. They put a bank of some ten telephones in a large meeting room and we all made calls based on a list of those who in the past four years, had not renewed. We had specific information on the cards and when we made contact, we updated as well as wrote down comments from those on the line. Finding people at home is one of the biggest problems for these calls as well as the current influx of telemarketing calls that complicates successful use of this method in recent years. BUT, it's one way that you might try to utilize and you can staff it with your volunteers. Again, a BIG THANKS at the end and some refreshments are welcome.

BOOSTER CLUB MEMBERS are usually especially good volunteers to help with special assignments. They are reliable and excited about being a part of the program. One thing with volunteers, DON'T EXPECT them to know EXACTLY how you want things done. This is new to many of them so you must have the evening or event CAREFULLY ORGANIZED (there's that word again) and SUPERVISED so that it's done correctly and efficiently and try to make it a fun event also.

Another very effective use of volunteers could be whenever you have a large mailing. One of your larger mailings could be your football season ticket flyers/information. You need people to stuff those envelopes and do it correctly. If it's basketball, you can call it "BIG STUFF" night. Set the hours as you need and make sure you have enough volunteers and work to go around plus enough THANKS at the end of the night.

I'm sure in your situation you have several very large events whereby you could effectively utilize volunteers. Your school's service clubs might also be available to help. If you just keep asking around, you can come up with different groups who would be most eager to assist. There are usually church groups and seniors that are available for the asking. It's another case of being creative to fill a need – and a very large need as the case may be. The larger the task, whether it be mail-outs or phone-a-thons or any other large special event, the volunteer route might be the best way to go.

Another use of volunteers could be your organization of an "ADVISORY BOARD FOR MARKETING" or Advisory Staff. This group could include "money" people; people of influence; celebrities, high-tech and computer people, attorneys, etc. This group could be available by just picking up the phone and getting some advice/ideas/opinions as you need them.

There might be an opportunity to establish a marketing class — one specifically for sports marketing — in your school. Make sure it's a two-semester class and if you can, require the successful completion of a summer project, as a grade requirement. A portion of the project might be to put in so many hours during the summer to help get ready for the upcoming football, soccer, or field hockey season with all its marketing needs. If you don't have this already, and you feel that it would be a terrific help to your marketing, write up a syllabus (you can get some ideas from other schools that have such a class), include a budget, objectives, class credits, etc., and present it to your administrators for possible approval for the beginning of the next school year. You'll need to list selling points and benefits to the students and the need for such a class. This marketing class could do some very important projects that would be most helpful to you and your marketing program. You could come up with lots of research that would improve everything from getting more students to attend games, to improving interest in a particular sport, to getting out the "good word" to more people, coming up with "special nights" and anything that might increase interest and sales – all would be most worthwhile and not busy work.

    Another excellent use of volunteers would be on game nights as ushers and ticket takers. As with all your staff, pre-season meetings discussing various duties and responsibilities including review of job description are in order. Other possibilities might include telephone coverage at certain times of the day when the student interns might not be available. Careful selection of personnel is always a MUST.

NOTES

CHAPTER 7

MAKE EACH NIGHT/DAY A SPECIAL EVENT — YOU ARE THE PRODUCER

In making each night or day (game/contest) a special event, this is another area that takes lots of preliminary planning and organization. You're going to need help on this one also. I have often mentioned at coaching clinics, that I never wanted to play a game without a pep band and cheerleaders. I'm sure every football coach will tell you how important the marching band, cheerleaders and cheering fans are to his team's success. At most schools where I coached, I would spend an hour pre-season visiting with the pep band at their practice session — first and foremost, to let them know how important and appreciated they were and secondly, to just answer questions about the team and have a fun exchange. From time to time, we would have an open house type of practice session where we would invite the pep band, cheerleaders and mascot. We would do the same for our final team banquet. The mascot was always a big hit. All of these people make for your event being an entertaining one.

> **What you strive for is to make the event as entertaining and the fans as comfortable as possible from the time they enter the parking lot to the time they leave.**

What you strive for is to make the event as entertaining and the fans as comfortable as possible from the time they enter the parking lot to the time they leave. Your restrictions as to what you can do at each event will be limited by your time, money, creative ideas and planning; and possibly administrative approval. The latter is the basis for your reputation; in this day and age of "the bizarre sells" — do your events/ideas with class. You'll last longer this way. Also, "BEWARE OF THE ACTIVITY TRAP" — don't confuse being busy with being productive — carefully THINK things out before you use them.

> **"BEWARE OF THE ACTIVITY TRAP" — don't confuse being busy with being productive**

Let's start at the beginning — make every effort to have your customers comfortable when they arrive — you have clearly marked parking areas and you have an easy flow of traffic coming in to your stadium/arena. A detailed MAP should be sent out to all season ticket holders prior to the season. Since you get one ounce for 34¢ — fill up the remainder of that ounce with other information on upcoming athletic events. This is also a good opportunity to first, say THANKS for being a season ticket holder, and then getting in a comment regarding their using their tickets. I've advocated, particularly in basketball, where you might have sixteen or seventeen home games, that IF you were unable to attend one of the games, that they give their tickets to a friend who might become a fan and potential season ticket-holder. I believe in basketball, you should follow up with another letter, this time from the head coach, asking them to do the same. This way you have an opportunity to build your season-ticket base plus you will have more people in those seats, more spending at concessions, and the beat goes on.

Then as your fans walk into the arena/stadium, you want to make it easy to find their seats. Smiling and helpful and friendly ticket takers help your cause. Just one grouch makes it the start of a dismal night for over a hundred or so customers. Then to the ushers again, kind, helpful, considerate, and friendly, and then you have the start of a good night. The same goes for their trip to the concession stands. Then there's some pre-game entertainment and watching the players warm-up. HOW ABOUT SOME TYPE OF GAME PROGRAM? I know in many instances they lose money

> **BUT try to have something available for the fans so they know the players from BOTH teams and can identify with them.**

BUT try to have something available for the fans so they know the players from BOTH teams and can identify with them. If it's just a piece of paper with the roster, opponents, and any advertising or news on specific players, statistics, and other news – add some nice computer art, a team photo, and add on as you see fit.

You and your game manager should be looking for any situations that need improvement. I believe you both have to "manage by walking around" – actually, <u>carefully</u> looking around when you do this. Have your glasses on — see problem areas and fix these as soon as you can. If your concession stands are too crowded – how about alleviating the problem by adding a small kiosk stand that handles just drinks and popcorn. Anything that will reduce the "standing in line" wait is going to help. You don't want to give fans an opportunity to complain – some will do it soon enough.

> **You don't want to give fans an opportunity to complain – some will do it soon enough.**

In basketball, utilize those time-outs for "sponsored" fan entertainment. If you have a Jumbotron – lots can be done with this. Otherwise, anything that has competition between fans, whether it be a type of shoot-out or whatever, goes over well. The only problem is that you don't want to do the same thing over and over again. Always be on the lookout for any type of quick-hitting time-out entertainment that you can find. Make sure you don't go over the time allotment — when that horn blows, off that court quickly. Remember you've probably got the band playing and the cheerleaders working. I would like to see cheerleaders get back to what they were originally intended to do — and that is LEAD CHEERS. If you have a dance team – great. But cheerleaders need to be involved in getting the fans cheering for their team — and the mascot can be a big help by going up in the stands and helping get the fans more into the action.

A very important part of the game is the ANNOUNCER. This person can be most helpful in everything you do. It's best to be on good terms with the announcer and let him/her know what's coming up and that you could use his/her help. An enthusiastic and fired up announcer is a big help. Don't be afraid to compliment this key person ... ditto for the scorer's table staff.

Now we get to half-time. You have various announcements that can be made and then it's quickly time for the half-time SHOW/ENTERTAINMENT. Make it just that. You'll probably need to audition various groups that are interested in performing — you'll need to take and make the time to do this.

Two areas of great importance, we have not forgotten. First, the singing or playing of the National Anthem. This again requires auditions and recommendations. You need a microphone and audio system that are top

> **I would like to see cheerleaders get back to what they were originally intended to do — and that is LEAD CHEERS.**

> **An enthusiastic and fired up announcer is a big help.**

notch. You can mix it up between the band playing the National Anthem or utilizing a singer. In both cases, let them know it's a basketball game and not a try-out performance. They need to keep in a certain time frame and be good.

Next and very important would be your communications with your radio people. They can be terrific at marketing your future opponents. Make sure they are good "cheerleaders" for your program and team. You and your media relations people should provide them with a steady stream of accurate statistics and material for use throughout the game. Their half-time guest is very important also — make sure they are set up in advance and that it is a very informative half-time guest. There should be a steady stream of pumping up that next game and particularly the next home game — "seats still available" and ticket information/locations, and the full nine yards.

Your game management people will make sure both teams get their five-minute warning to get back on the field/court in time for the second half to begin. Providing officials with a separate locker/dressing area and proper security is a must. Also your game manager can help avoid conflicts between teams and officials by having locker rooms spread out so all three go in separate and opposite directions at half time and end of game. By keeping them all separate, you can avoid potential problems.

> **There should be a steady stream of pumping up that next game and particularly the next home game**

> **Providing officials with a separate locker/dressing area and proper security is a must.**

By the way, we had a pre-game entrance at Northwestern University in basketball that was somewhat different. The pep band arrived by every band member coming in a different entrance and running with their instruments through the arena and to their assigned area and began playing immediately. It also helps to have a band director who's really into it also. Coordinated efforts between the band and the cheerleaders can really help the fans get into the game. It's always a nice gesture that there is coordinated cheering between the band, cheerleaders, and fans when the team comes out to warm-up and when they come back on the field/arena for the start of the game. Add some pizzazz. Help get that team psyched and ready to go all out.

And now we start the second half — the announcer has given out the half-time statistics and possibly scores from around the league and away we go into the 2nd half — more of the same — need that band playing and playing. The cheers for defense are really helpful – coordinated by the cheerleaders.

A very effective and appreciated gimmick is the throwing of t-shirts into the fans when a three-point goal is scored in basketball. Also, with the shooting of t-shirts in the air to fans — particularly with those with the t-shirts encouraging more noise; this is another exciting gimmick for games. When the game is over, and I hope it's a win, you'll now have everyone trying to leave the event at one time. Let's look at a few ideas that might keep some of the fans around so that perhaps, only half of the crowd will be headed to their cars and on to the roads, at one time. Recently at a Houston Astros game at Enron Field, they had a popular band/group perform immediately after the game. It looked to me that about 5,000 fans stayed around after the game to listen.

In women's basketball, Texas Tech University, for a long time, has had a separate meeting with the fans almost immediately after their games. Coach Marsha Sharp and her staff do a terrific job with this. As the game ends, and all the players and coaches go to their locker room, fans move to center court seats on a specific side of the arena while a lectern, P.A. system/sound system is set up at mid-court. One of the assistants eventually comes out to initiate the proceedings allowing Coach Sharp time to do her radio show and come out to talk to the fans. She will bring along one or two players with her to speak to the crowd. I've witnessed about ten of these post-game sessions with the fans and I was most impressed. The coach that initiates the session can spend some time going over stats or game highlights while giving Coach Sharp that additional time with the team. I would say that after some games, half the crowd stayed for this. This is a big boost to spreading out the departure of all those cars because many games they had over 10,000 fans in attendance.

    I am sure the above can be done in all sports — you have to build it slowly. In football or soccer, you could have the above event take place indoors in an auditorium or whatever, however, its probably most effective when it happens within ten minutes after the game. At the University of Utah in basketball when I was there we started to "pipe in" to the arena my post-game radio show in an attempt to hold some of the fans in their seats or on the concourse/concession stands. We also, within about 10-12 minutes immediately following the game, would hand out a one-page "Most Valuable Ute" flyer. It was simply a one page, previously printed with "Most Valuable Ute," Best Free Throw Shooter, Assist Leader, Most Steals, and whatever you want to hype. One assistant coach would go immediately to the Sports Information Office, taking along a copy of the final stats, and would take it to the copy machine — the headings were already printed in; and they would just fill in the specific names of the winners in each category basically from the stat sheet and the assistant would give them the name of the most valuable Ute. We started to get more kids hanging around to get a copy of this — one more delay in having all 12,000 people leaving the arena at the

> **Remember on the way in, they're probably all coming in within a 30-45 minute window — going out it's all at once.**

same time. Remember on the way in, they're probably all coming in within a 30-45 minute window — going out it's all at once.

Now once you've taken yourself and the fan through an entire game from coming in to the arena/stadium until that person drives out — how can you improve on this the next time. ANALYSIS — ANALYSIS — ANALYSIS

In football, tailgating is such a big social event — particularly with the colleges. You can build on this in your situation. If you're just trying it out, start small and then build on it. Get a "core" group of boosters to come early, barbecue, socialize, to start out in the parking lot, then work to get more for the next home game, and you can start to really get a crowd in a short time. You might try it with basketball except with the colder weather in many areas it could work in an adjacent indoor area. It's a great social event and a building of school spirit.

To make your game a special event, really work on the INTRODUCTION OF THE HOME TEAM; coordinate with the

> **Make that intro big time.**

announcer and cheerleaders. Make that intro big time. If indoors, lights dim, band playing, student pep group fired up, cheerleaders leading the way, hand clapping, cheering, yelling, with perhaps the mascot leading the team out or

> **... it's show time.**

the head coach — it's show time. Depending on the league rules for noisemakers — clappers, and the like — if the rules allow, you can help provide them for that first game. It's good in football, to have the marching band put on a post-game show; that helps to keep some of the people in the stands and concessions selling.

Now keep a list of possibilities for half-time shows for each of your sports. In basketball, keep notes on 3 by 5 cards on different events you can stage during time-outs that will provide entertainment for the fans. Get your new ideas from networking with your buddies in marketing and also by watching games on TV and also coming up with ideas of your own that will fit your situation.

You can always work around half-time shows by honoring someone of a past championship team. If you honor these and/or a celebrity, with advance advertising it will create more advance publicity and can be a "draw" to help increase attendance. It's a nice gesture — and generally it's of interest to the fans and of course, the media gets something different to feature.

SAMPLE ORGANIZATIONAL WORKSHEET

SPORT: _____

Date/Time OPPONENT	Halftime	Time-Outs	GiveAways Promotions	Groups	Functions (Nat'l Anthem)	Functions Pre & Post	Misc.
MISC. NOTES							

The following program was set up at Northwestern University in the early 1990s — you can adapt and adopt and get ideas from this and utilize in your own program. It was very popular.

"SHOOT FOR REEBOKS" Program

Coach Bill Foster
Head Basketball Coach
Northwestern University
Evanston, IL 60208

This program (half-time) proved to be very entertaining, lively and of little expense to the sponsors -- REEBOK -- using maybe fifteen gift certificates that would be given to each "winning" participant, who would in turn, fill out and send in and receive his or her pair of shoes free within four to six weeks.

Approximately seven minutes before the half, students who wanted to participate would begin to line up in single file near the entrance adjacent to our Pep Band. One director would call out to the next participant (limited to students only -- but next year may include adult volunteers, etc.) to attempt a shot from beyond the top of the key (approximately a 20 foot shot). If the shot was made, they would receive a gift certificate for a free pair of Reeboks. If missed, the next would run out and receive the basketball and take his or her turn...this goes on for an allotted number of minutes.

The fans started to get into it -- loud cheering when shots were made and even boos when missed, etc. Even the Pep Band gets into it. Students even chanted "Reebok!! Reebok!!" etc. at times, particularly after it got going.

For Reebok, a full page ad in the game program stating the purpose and Reebok and the dates of the games in which this contest would be a part of the half-time activities.

The contest received TV coverage during our ESPN games and other Big Ten Network games (some also on FNN SCORE -- a total of twenty televised games). The PA Announcer and Message Board were also "promo"ing it. Free radio plugs on the NU Basketball Network were given and announced during the half-time coverage including the name of sponsor, etc.

IN ADDITION . . . on our Coaches Show (weekly) we ran a feature on the "Shoot for Reeboks" Activity and also devoted one segment to the Reebok Coaches Clinic held on the Northwestern campus in early October.

Boise State* • Fresno State • Hawaii
Louisiana Tech* • Nevada • Rice • San Jose State
SMU • TCU • UTEP • Tulsa

WAC Member July, 2001

FROM BILL FOSTER (10/29/99) MEMO:

SOME MARKETING THOUGHTS FOR THE HOLIDAYS -- FROM MY MARKETING GURU, DAN KENNEDY OUT OF PHOENIX, AZ. I SUBSCRIBE TO SEVERAL OF HIS NEWSLETTERS/PUBLICATIONS AND HE RANKS RIGHT UP THERE WITH "THE BEST" ...

TIME TO GEAR UP SEASONAL & YEAR-END PROMOTIONS.

Santa Claus is comin' - ally or enemy? I can't even begin to describe how much I detested the fat man when I was broke and scrambling to make the bucks I needed for last month's bills. I never figured out how to make Santa an ally. In my businesses, he was always the enemy, clouding peoples' minds, sucking up their dollars, and pretty much throwing a giant monkey wrench into my ability to make money for a good 8 to 10 weeks. Later, as soon as I could afford it, I basically surrendered, and took tons of time off from Thanksgiving until mid-January. Still do. For me, he's too formidable a competitor to wrestle. If you happen to be in one of the rare businesses like mine that Christmas season darned near cripples, you've got my sympathy. My suggestion is shut down and find a beach you like. Fortunately, most businesses can prosper with Santa's help. For some, he can be a moneymaking juggernaut. In any case, here is a simple, inarguable fact of life: beginning about mid-November and continuing, with ascending intensity, until Christmas virtually every consumer and most businesspeople have everything related to "the holidays" on their mind, actually using up all their mental capacity — so if you do **not** link your business, products, services, offers and communication to "the holidays", you are dead.

THANKSGIVING presents a fantastic marketing opportunity for most businesses - it's a non-denominational event, hard to offend anybody's delicate sensiblities with it, and made-to-order for "thank you" promotions to past and present customers. If you can't create a cash flow surge out of that, you're badly in need of a brain transfusion.

And this time around we have this millenium stuff. As we get closer and closer, it will heat up. Just like people get eager for change, improvement, the new, different, better, at new years, those feelings'll be even stronger at the new millenium. How can you link what you sell to this desire and optimism and uncertainty about the new millenium?

Use all the holidays to your advantage as they can all be special events for your marketing**

9250 E. Costilla Ave., Suite 300
Englewood, CO 80112-3662
Phone: 303-799-9221 FAX: 303-799-3888
www.wacsports.com

NOTES

NOTES

CHAPTER 8
IMPORTANT EXTRAS TO GET YOU OVER THE TOP — SPECIAL IDEAS TO GET <u>STUDENTS</u> OUT TO YOUR GAMES

There are many extras that you can utilize to help you sell seats including special pricing. We'll address some of those in this chapter. First, is convenience ... this would apply from the time you purchase your tickets to the convenience of getting to the game and into the arena/stadium. Second would be special incentives to purchase tickets and/or be the recipient of

> **I like the "SUPPORT YOUR HOME TOWN TEAM".**

reduced or ticket give-aways. Special campaigns have slogans that feature the team and its season — I like the "SUPPORT YOUR HOME TOWN TEAM". Another feature is the comparative pricing of tickets to your games to those of local professional teams if they are nearby. You are constantly working to get your team publicity and features. You work to get a brand identity.

Before the game begins, the fan gets to feel the excitement of pre-game ceremonies, and from the national anthem to the final whistle/gun; you're watching young people really compete at an amateur level. You also are part of the excitement generated by the student body. This enthusiasm is contagious. You're selling great family entertainment and being with your friends and their kids. You are providing something for everyone. You get to know the players and you get to see good sportsmanship and enthusiasm on the field/court as opposed to players going through their warm-ups in slow motion. This makes it all the more exciting. You may not see as much spectacular play but you'll see quite a show. Chances are you'll see your neighbors and be able to watch their kids play. The half-times and time-outs will be interesting and you'll get into the game more and more as you go.

> **You also are part of the excitement generated by the student body. This enthusiasm is contagious.**

Teams/schools that provide pre-and or post-game socials or both present not only a nice family atmosphere but give a wonderful opportunity for attendees to socialize and network. You have your tailgating as a big social event prior to football games and after games also. For games in the evenings, many of the workers come directly from work and don't have an opportunity to stop at some crowded restaurant for dinner – so you provide the answer – and he/she can meet the rest of the family to eat. The local restaurants won't think its such a great idea BUT "you do what you gotta do".

Many of the minor league baseball and hockey teams do a great job with their game programs with everything included in the program. Some have maps of the refreshment stands, birthday party programs, parking directory, listing of special nights including give-aways, the fan's guide to the ballpark or arena, composite schedule of all the league teams, the various community relations programs, and a host of other pieces of information including not only player rosters, but players' pictures, biographical sketches, upcoming home games and the complete works.

While we're on game programs, you should try to involve all your vendors with taking out advertisements with you. You should make sure you have a large distribution of the programs as well as sales of the same. You can put extra programs to good use by sending out to potential fans, which in turn gives your advertisers more exposure locally. You never throw an old game program away — you give them away to potential new advertisers and

> **Teams/schools that provide pre-and or post-game socials or both present not only a nice family atmosphere but give a wonderful opportunity for attendees to socialize and network.**

fans and you keep just a few for your files. One way to help sales is to have a lucky number winner with the number inside the game program. You can make it a production by using a local celebrity or well-known person to handle the drawing at an appropriate time during the game.

WALMART has "greeters" at most all of their stores as you come in and pick up your cart. DEVELOP YOUR ENTIRE STAFF TO BE GREETERS and GREETER FRIENDLY.

DEVELOP YOUR ENTIRE STAFF TO BE GREETERS and GREETER FRIENDLY.

I really don't believe you have to have "give-aways" to get people in the seats. It's a nice extra. Most professional teams have close to a full schedule of give-aways all the *way* from pens, to key chains, caps, jerseys, t-shirts, visors, baseball cards, and the like. Companies do like this way to advertise – of course, thrown in with this is scoreboard advertising, program ads, announcements during the game; to give the advertiser more bang for the buck. I do believe, in certain situations, that this kind of incentive can be helpful.

A very popular give-away now are TELEPHONE CARDS. They, also, are very popular in FUND RAISING.

A very popular give-away now are TELEPHONE CARDS. They, also, are very popular in FUND RAISING. These cards can give you ten minutes to whatever number you want, of anytime, anywhere free calls. They also provide advertising on the card as well as your own personal message after you dial the number (and this can be changed when you so desire), giving extra exposure. One of the selling points is that everyone should have one in their wallet/purse to always have in case of emergency. We've provided at the end of this chapter some specific information on these coming from CommCard USA. A friend of mine, Paul Rizzo of Rizzo Associates, out of Lake Geneva, WI (262) 248-0880, has been telling me about the popularity of these cards for several years.

FACILITY NAMING RIGHTS occur more and more today. The income from this can be extremely profitable and inviting. It gives a business the right to have their name on the new field/arena. High school and colleges are more involved with this now. It's an excellent way to get large sums of income. The same goes for pricing out parts of the facility like the scoreboard, locker room, equipment and training rooms, classrooms, etc. with schools.

Texas Christian University, Fort Worth, Texas, printed a nice flyer entitled, "Here's The Pitch for Team 100" —TCU is looking to field an All-Star Team 100 to help build one of the Metroplex's most outstanding baseball facilities and to at last give the Horned Frogs the stadium they deserve ... a contribution of $25,000 and joining team 100 (they give five years to complete the gift). Included are four season tickets for five years (baseball); permanent recognition in the stadium and a chance to win a PT

Cruiser. They also specify that amounts for the naming "opportunities" for Suites ($150,000 – five years}; Bullpens (two at $100,000) the Dugouts, coaches field office, radio booths, etc.

In late July it was reported that FedEx had offered to pay as much as $120 million dollars to call the new NBA team in Memphis, the Memphis Express and attire the players in their orange and purple colors. At the time of this printing, the NBA had said "no". It will be interesting to follow the progress of this. There are many who feel that the sports industry should be allowed to use this revenue stream to minimize the public's costs.

What happens when your team is NOT expected to have a great year; and perhaps isn't that exciting? This presents a larger challenge to you – the marketing director. That's why pre-season HYPE is important to selling your season tickets early; as well as selling your single games as far in advance as possible. So much can go wrong with a team during the season; so it's important that you get started early and often on HYPING THAT TEAM, COACH, PLAYERS, expectations – while they are still undefeated. A problem, to be sure, is that not everybody is ready for the season very far in advance. But it's AN OPPORTUNITY for you to show your stuff. Not everyone is going to be undefeated so pick out any bright spots for the season and DWELL ON THAT – SELL. Timing is important as to how far in

That's why pre-season HYPE is important to selling your season tickets early; as well as selling your single games as far in advance as possible.

advance you should start your ticket campaign — BUT SELLING has no season as it's a twelve month a year "opportunity". Timing on this becomes an "educated" guess.

There are many ideas to HYPE UP the upcoming season in the months prior to that first game. One is to conduct a clinic for coaches; or a clinic/camp for players/one for parents/fans/students, and the like. A pre-season scrimmage allowing fan attendance can be a plus. The Spring football games have taken on a different look lately. Many coaches, fearing the injury possibilities, have adjusted this annual event. "Special nights" pre-season utilizing a special celebrity as host might work well. We did a neat thing in basketball at Northwestern University with a "Night With Dick Vitale and the Wildcats". Dick did his usual excellent job with lots of enthusiasm and the evening included dunk contests, three-point shooting events, Dick's own player introductions and a short full-court scrimmage. In basketball, it's easy to tie in this type of event after a football game at home. One caution here is that you don't want to make your event too long. The fans would be at the football game for three hours and then be faced with sitting through another two-hour sporting event. The objection generally is that it's too long a day/night.

> **BUT SELLING has no season as it's a twelve month a year "opportunity".**

Any type of "pre-season tease" type of program, whether it be a practice session, scrimmage, luncheon, breakfast, or the sort – is helpful in providing more interest in your team. It's one more OPPORTUNITY to have a "captive" audience to SELL – SELL – SELL. Anything that adds to this like having a player sing the National Anthem, or having a media member coach the team, combined with an autograph session or alumni game is an added attention grabber and should be utilized.

While we're on "important extras to get you over the top", always be on the look-out to improve every phase of your operation. One area to check out closely is your telephone service. Whether it be calling in to order tickets or just trying to get information, this is a great way to GAIN a customer or LOSE a customer. Today people are getting sick and tired of going through the "automatic messages hell" that many of today's businesses experience. You know the one where you have nine options, all nicely recorded to waste the caller's time. If there is a way to lose a customer, it's the automatic recorded messages with all those options and the lack of being able to talk to someone personally to solve a problem. I know it's the cost of having people answering the phones, but it's too easy in athletics for a potential customer to just say "forget it" and stay home and watch something on TV – and save not only time but money as well. You've seen the advertisements, we're employing

Today people are getting sick and tired of going through the "automatic messages hell" that many of today's businesses experience.

"happy and cheerful" people. Ditto for you with all your people involved in the management of an event. Don't forget to keep your employees happy and FEELING IMPORTANT. Everyone that comes in contact with the FANS can be your greatest public relations ASSETS or your PUBLIC RELATIONS DISASTERS.

As an important aside to your program, you might be able to add some important extras to what you are doing by helping the athletes themselves. Your teams should be encouraged and placed in speech classes. How about in junior high and again, in senior high – and of course, in college. With all the media attention and requirements, it should be a class taken in the first semester of the freshman year, in college.

In addition, some one in media relations or your English department or speech, should have a special class(es) set up to better prepare players for exposure to print media, radio and television. You can set up a TV camera, have a reporter come in to your classroom, and do actual "live" interviews and have a critique of the performance by the player. There are a lot of little hints that will help athletes in their early years of their career. Your outstanding players are involved with intense media scrutiny, and this gives them experience and preparation for getting polished at what will be upcoming for them. You would be getting them "media ready".

> **Their parents should be notified of your school's concern and what you are doing to assist in their development.**

These "mock" interviews will prove to be valuable for your athletes. They won't volunteer to do this in all probability. But your school's concern for their well-being is an important part of their education. Their parents should be notified of your school's concern and what you are doing to assist in their development. The critique and review by someone well qualified is a most important part of this process.

The following "Quacker Backer — Smart Card Holder Information" flyer is from Howard Cornfield, QUAD CITY MALLARDS ICE HOCKEY TEAM, in the United Hockey League. They do an excellent job of marketing and have large crowds in attendance – one of the best averages and percentages of total number of seats, in minor league sports. Howard is a real worker, very creative, and is an excellent manager. He's one of the bright stars out there. Along with this information flyer, came a very attractive four-color brochure explaining the entire program in detail. It showed pictures of items/merchandise that the loyal fans could receive through this Fan Loyalty Rewards Program. There were plenty of attractive items to choose from all the way from notepads and pucks to leather jackets with plenty in-between. I particularly liked the various automatic incentives when you reached 100 points, 200 points, 300 points (exclusive skate with the Mallards for all members reaching 300 points regardless of redemptions), at 400 points (free

Quacker Backer Log Puck to all members reaching 400 points regardless of redemptions) up to 500 points (Exclusive 500 club gift; on-ice presentation and sponsor gift package). Terrific incentives including a free one night stay at the Fairfield Inn in Moline or Davenport.

You can use this idea to your advantage as these programs become more and more popular like the frequent flyer airline miles.

Quacker Backer – Smart Card Holder Information

Attend the first four Mallard home games — **October 14, October 21, October 28, November 4** — and earn bonus dollars (between $5-$20 depending on your ticket package) on your MARK smart card.

How?

Quacker Backer/Smart Card holders need to:

- Attend the first four Mallard home games and swipe your card as you enter through the turnstiles.
- Stop by The MARK box office between **November 8 and December 9** during regular business hours. **(Offer expires December 9, 2000.)**
- Bring your smart card and a valid driver's license
- The box office will verify that you attended all four games and will load your card with bonus dollars to be used at any concession stand during any event at The MARK!

* **Please note:** Your free bonus dollars can **only** be loaded at the box office — **not** at the Smart Card booth located at the top of the stairs during events. Due to ticket traffic, bonus dollars **cannot** be loaded between 5:30-7:30 on game nights.

> **Regular Box Office Hours:** Monday-Friday: 10:00 a.m.—5:30 p.m.
> Saturday: 10:00 a.m.—2:00 p.m.

Lost or Stolen Cards

- Lost or stolen cards will be replaced one time free of charge. Subsequent lost or stolen cards will result in a $5 replacement fee.
- Although cards are replaceable, **we will not be able to replace the cash value remaining on the card**.
- Replacement cards will need to have a new dollar amount loaded onto the card at the card owner's expense to receive the additional card benefits.

Remember

- Your Quacker Backer/Smart Card must have value on it to receive the additional card benefits including early admittance.
- Your card is reloadable — when you run out of value just add whatever dollar amount you prefer (in $5 increments up to $500) at The MARK box office or the Smart Card booth during events. Cash, check, or credit card accepted.
- Your Quacker Backer/Smart card allows you to receive valuable discounts at area merchants.

In addition to your bonus dollars, Quacker Backer/Smart Card holders can also receive valuable discounts on other upcoming MARK events. Show your smart card at The MARK box office today and receive:

- $4.00 off tickets to the TJ Maxx Tour of World Gymnastics Champions—October 29
- $3.00 off tickets to The Andy Williams Christmas Show—December 15
- Watch for future discounted shows.
- Discounts are not available on arena club tickets purchased through the Mallards office in advance of the public on-sale.

Stop by the box office or smart card booth located at the top of the steps during events with questions or concerns.

QUACKER BACKER
FAN LOYALTY REWARDS PROGRAM

PROGRAM HIGHLIGHTS

- Membership is FREE! All you need is a completely filled out application for each ticket that you own.
- Earn points toward great merchandise and prizes just for being a loyal Mallards fan!
- Receive special offers from local businesses created exclusively for Quacker Backer/SmartCard members!
- This program includes a fully reloadable MARK SmartCard for buying food and beverages at the arena!

ANSWERS TO SOME OF YOUR QUESTIONS

What is the "Quacker Backer" program?
This program is designed to reward Mallards fans for being such loyal supporters. This fan loyalty rewards program allows you to accumulate points onto your membership card. These points are redeemable for exclusive Quacker Backer merchandise, autographed items, and valuable coupons good at area businesses.

How can I become a member?
In its inaugural season, only Mallards Season Ticketholders will be offered membership into the Quacker Backer Program. In order to activate your membership, you will need to complete a Quacker Backer application form (which has been mailed to you). You can mail, fax or bring in the completed application to the Mallards office. Or you can apply on-line at: www.qcmallards.com/quackerbacker/application You can pick up your card when you bring in your completed application after October 10, 2000.

I have multiple season tickets in my name. Do I need to fill out applications for all of them?
We recognize that many Season Ticketholders purchase multiple seats, whether for their families, businesses, etc. We do, however, need you to fill out one application per season ticket. We understand that certain portions of the application will not be applicable for children, but please fill out each application to the best of your ability.

How do I earn points?
There are many different ways to earn Quacker Backer points. The easiest of which is to come to Mallards home games. Each time you enter The MARK for a Mallards home game, there will be terminals at the turnstiles. Insert your card and you will receive points just for coming to the game. You can also earn points by purchasing Mallards merchandise at the Mallard's Nest, bringing a group to a Mallards game, or by visiting local sponsors on a "Quacker Backer Spot" promotion.

What will I do with all these points?
This is where the real rewards are! As you collect Quacker Backer points, you can redeem them for special prizes! The back of this brochure highlights some of the great prizes that we have available this season! NOTE: To choose your prize(s) and redeem your points, bring your card into The Mallard's Nest, located at 1509 3rd Avenue A, Moline.

Will this card also be my MARK SmartCard?
Yes! The MARK of the Quad Cities and the Mallards have combined these two programs onto just one card. This card is now a fully reloadable SmartCard that can be used to buy concessions at any MARK event. If you have additional questions about the SmartCard, please contact Laurie Hammill at The MARK (764-2001, ext. 330).

Does this card do anything else for me?
Yes! This card will earn you special discounts at local businesses and will be your pass to exclusive Mallards events. It will also earn you $1 off parking in The MARK parking lot and VIP SmartCard Status for MARK events. In the future, this card will have many more exciting features as well, including becoming your actual season ticket next season!

What if I lose my card?
Not to worry! Just check in at the Quacker Backer Table or visit the Mallard's office during business hours to get a new card. It will be FREE the first time you lose it, and only $5 for any additional replacements.

Are there any special promotions that I should know about?
Yes! If you attend the first four Mallards home games (regardless of your ticket plan), you will be eligible to receive credit on your SmartCard. Full season ticket holders will receive $20, Weekend and Holiday plan holders will receive $15, 21-game plan holders will receive $10, and 11-game plan holders will receive $5.

SCHEDULE OF POINTS AWARDED

10 POINTS — Each Mallards Home Game

5 POINTS — Extra for Home Games played Monday - Thursday (Holidays excluded)

1 POINT — For every $5 spent at The Mallard's Nest (rounded to the nearest 5 points)

5 POINT — For every 10 people brought to a Mallards Home Game in a Group booked through the Mallard's office

25 POINTS OR MORE — Visiting a "Quacker Backer Spot" (These spots will take place at local businesses throughout the season. Each spot will be unique to the location and points may vary. Details will follow on upcoming Quacker Backer Spot locations.)

??? POINTS — New things will become available throughout the season. Look for details!

QUESTIONS & ADDITIONAL INFORMATION

If you have any additional questions or need information regarding the Quacker Backer program, contact Julie Germeraad, Director of Fan Card Operations/ Marketing at (309) 764-7825 or send an email to julie@qcmallards.com.

> As a coach, I didn't show the same respect and importance to this important part of the game.

Being involved for several years with game management with the Southwest Conference, the Big 12 and the Western Athletic Conference – I have the two-page newsletter/memo that I sent out to each of our school's game managers on December 18, 2000. As a coach, I didn't show the same respect and importance to this important part of the game. I've since asked that at least one member of the coaching staff be involved in these meetings and in the planning that is done prior to the season. Any problems with crowd control can be damaging to the school's reputation and should not be taken lightly. The same goes for mechanical problems that might delay a game.

Here's a true-false test with just two questions:

Two Misnomers —   (1)   Winning and championships bring crowds
                   (2)   Build it and they will come

<u>GETTING MORE STUDENTS OUT TO YOUR GAMES</u>: This portion should probably be in a separate chapter because it's SO IMPORTANT. The students at games are so very important in many ways. First is their cheering and their enthusiasm for the team/game. Second, is they are very creative in their cheers and spontaneity. Thirdly, they usually stick with their team through the bad times as well as the good times. Fourth, it's part of the

NOTES

educational process and an important part of their social life. Fifth, they like to have fun and provide entertainment to the fans and so on. It's a fact, you really need them and I believe, TODAY, more than ever, we need to WORK to get them out. Of course, winning cures a lot of ills – a deep tradition really helps as it starts when they are freshmen in college – it's the place to be and they help to make it a "happening" place. This is another area where you need to be creative to get them to attend. Meeting with your students or having a <u>student advisory board</u>, will give you some better ideas to get their attention and attendance. Try to get a good balance of men/women, if college, dorm, fraternity, sorority, dayhops, etc. so all groups are represented.

Here's some thoughts/ideas:

1. In high schools, daily announcements over the P.A. system.

2. Have players talk (appeal) to their classmates (might as well add friends and parents) to come out and support their team.

3. Free (no charge to students); or if a charge, significantly lower prices. This will also depend upon the demand. Schools with large student bodies, and great teams, you probably have to get in to the lottery system. This is a nice problem.

4. Special one-game incentives; like free telephone cards, bobbleheads, items that are interesting and have value, and those that you probably

can get donated for your give-away.

5. End of game concerts with attractive and appealing musical groups.

6. Colleges, and even high schools, offer free bus transportation. You may be able to get a business to sponsor this.

7. Free end-of-game incentives — free t-shirts (sponsored, or course). During games, the "shooting" of t-shirts into the stands and particularly the student section, creates a lot of interest and enthusiasm.

8. Start "courting them" (students) at an early age with special "kids" program which include newsletters, e-mail and web site possibilities. Also, have them involved during the game in some way with the mascot or after the game. Rice University does a nice thing after a game with kids lining up to take free throws.

9. Social get-togethers; some free food will always be an attraction. You might want to do something AFTER the game to hold them there. If not the food at the event, a coupon that will enable them to get free fast food. Special price for a burger, fries, and a drink coupon would spark interest.

10. Special, Special, Special. I really liked what the University of Oklahoma women's team did several years ago. In one of those "Let's

Fill the Arena for the Largest Crowd To Ever See a Women's Game in The State of Oklahoma" — they did it. I was there in attendance and they won the game (a Big 12 contest) — with over 10,000 at the game, much in the way of festivities and promotion for this event.

Survey your game's starting times, if you have that option.

11. Survey your game's starting times, if you have that option. Also what days of the week are more attractive to students? Most leagues are locked in to specific days but your starting time might be adjusted to encourage more students AND FANS to attend.

12. Look at your schedule – is there any flexibility in attracting a team or two that might be more attractive to students. As you develop rivalries, this gets the attention of students.

13. Have special "Date Nights/Days", and come up with others that would be appealing to students.

"Cater" to students – don't just "expect" them to show up in droves.

14. "Cater" to students – don't just "expect" them to show up in droves. Even come up with a flyer especially for students to promote the team – THEIR TEAM. THEIR CLASSMATES.

15. Build cheering sections; have special section close to the floor and the team -"close to the action" is an excellent selling point as well as being with their friends/classmates.

16. You build student attendance like you do all of your fans – "ONE STUDENT AT A TIME" – "take a friend" and have student council-type groups come up with special ideas and attractions.

17. Have a pre-season exhibition game or scrimmage at a "time of the day/night" convenient for the students – "<u>package</u>" with something else to make it more interesting and appealing to them.

18. Have the coaches visit the student section; or any group meetings; or with colleges, go to the dorms, living groups, etc. and make their "pitch" and have a fun night with questions and answers. The coach can take a player or two along.

19. If you don't want to get a student advisory group together, just visit with a few students and "brainstorm" in a session with some refreshments. You'll come up with some special ideas that will be attractive. Ditto with members of the team, they've got some thoughts on this also.

20. Anything going home to parents (report cards; special notices, etc.), add pocket schedules that include any special promotions like "Parents' Day/Night" whereby the parents and the students will attend together.

> **You build student attendance like you do all of your fans – "ONE STUDENT AT A TIME"**

21. Special posters of the team are usually very popular. Utilize the "We Need You" approach with the finger pointing to YOU. Excellent for placement in hallways, classrooms, office walls, dorm rooms, and you name it. They particularly look good in the windows of stores and restaurants that are frequented by students.

22. Any special "signage" that you might be able to secure, to be placed in appropriate places on campus. Large signs located above the street is a possibility.

23. Any special "verbal" announcements that can be made. Work closely with your student radio station and get them on board with helping you get the word out about upcoming games. Make sure you get coaches and players to be available for interviews with the student station.

24. Make sure you are on any and all of the school's rotating message boards.

25. Development of a student PEP/CHEER club – special seating. Make sure they plan on being the most active cheering section at the game. Encourage their helping you get their friends out to the games and participating.

26. Try to involve students in many of your game night/day events where they can participate. In basketball, for example, involve students in those shooting contests, race car ride/races, shoot-out, competition. It's always good to have a member of the band or pep band involved as the rest of the band gets involved and those people are terrific fans.

27. Seasonal marketing tie-ins with the students, starting with New Year's Day going through the year to New Year's Eve. There are a large number of Holidays to utilize; also end of the semester game night, exams are over, welcome back after semesters, etc.

28. A student marketing campaign similar to: "Every student, get a new student to attend Saturday's game", etc.

29. Particularly in college, direct campaigns and attendance competition between fraternities and sororities, and living groups. High schools could adapt a similar competition between junior high schools (where there are more than one), etc.

30. Create "fun" events during the games like "Happy Birthday" night/day when a birthday falls on that day, band can play "Happy Birthday" and make it a big deal.

31. Special "meet the players and coaches" event just for students – have pictures/autograph session at same time.

32. All these special promotional events aimed at the students should get a lot of publicity in the school paper and any other media that you can reach. The same goes for a photographer that will get some special "shots" for the local paper and also the student paper.

33. If you have a student radio/TV station, help them get a sponsor to do a pre-season scrimmage or intra-squad game. This helps the station give some students pre-season experience with announcing/color, etc. BUT it also serves to get the message out to all who listen that your season is about to begin and other important information. Always a "see you at the game" announcement.

34. Special newsletter to all the students. These may be difficult to get around to everyone, but certainly not impossible. It's good to have the coach always comment on how important the students are to the team's success and should profile key team members and have a team picture. This is a good place to advertise how to obtain a team picture/poster.

35. You can utilize the above with "endorsements " by key members of the student body stating what a "fun time" and exciting time they've personally had at games.

36. Possibly set up a game or two "on the road" that through competition, the winners get to travel with the team.

37. Have a few of the most visible students do some commercials for the student radio station on how exciting it is to be a part of the game.

38. Have signage in all the student hang-outs on the upcoming games and the schedule, "be where your friends will be".

39. Be alert to "one thing leads to another" type of possibility. You see or hear about another school doing something similar and you adapt and adopt per your situation.

40. NETWORK with others in your field regarding student attendance. Usually schools OUT of your league are willing to share information as well as attending marketing event seminars that are available and affordable. Be ALERT in your reading, it's amazing how many magazines and/or newspaper articles will give you some EXCELLENT IDEAS that you can utilize.

41. If you are teaching a class, make it a priority to SELL students within your class. If you can speak to any teachers/professors in your business department or marketing classes about assigning projects that will help you – such a project might be to do a study of how we might get more students to our games, etc. Teachers/professors many

times, are more than willing to be helpful with a meaningful and needed project like this.

42. Special post-game reception(s) for different student groups that attend – sponsored of course.

Put the **Fun** back into **Fun**draising

Custom Designed Phone Cards Provide Effective, Efficient, and Rewarding Results

Long distance calling time is a universal premium gift. Everyone can find value, and most will call their friends and family. CommCard USA has proven that custom designed phone cards will provide a very unique and rewarding fundraising opportunity for your group or organization

What's the big deal with using phone cards?

Example:

A high school soccer team wanted to raise funds to cover expenses for their weekend tournaments. CommCard USA printed their team picture onto phone cards. Each card had 60-minutes of calling time and a special thank you message from the team (heard when the card is used). Each player was to sell 10 cards. They did, and quickly, as most went directly to family and friends. Exciting for the players to sell their own phone card. Rewarding to family and friends as a unique keepsake and useful gift. Their funds were raised.

P. S. Some players also used their cards to call home while from they're out of town tournaments.

There are many creative ways to use phone cards for raising funds, however, it starts with the simple fact that people will use the long distance calling time. Most of us make long distance phone calls, and even if you only pay .07 per minute, read the small print, and you'll see that the .07 per minute applies only between stipulated hours, with residential to residential calling only, certain restrictions may apply, and it's available in *most* areas. People will use the phone cards.

Custom Designed Card Image:
An exciting aspect to the phone cards is the custom designed card image. From 1-color to 4-color process, we can produce any image that you desire. It is perfect for any keepsake images or photographs, ideal for special emblems or logos, and a very important impact for any sponsors or coop partners. The custom designed phone card is literally your pocket-sized billboard.

Custom Audio Message:
CommCard USA phone cards also come with your own custom audio message. The message is heard with each card use, and because it works just like voice-mail, you can record, change, or update your audio message at any time. It is an excellent opportunity to personally say thank you. It is also a terrific impact for any sponsors or coop partners.

Custom Audio Message Example:
"Thank you from everyone at XYZ, we sincerely appreciate your efforts. XYZ would also like to invite you to our fall festival on Saturday, the 21st. We will have lots of food, fun, and entertainment, and we hope you can join us. Again, thank you for your support".

As a premium gift or fundraising product, phone cards provide a fresh alternative.

Create Your Own Phone Cards in 3 Simple Steps

Step 1
Design a card image. From 1-color to 4-color process, CommCard USA will produce your image onto durable plastic cards.

Step 2
Record your own audio message. It works just like voice-mail and CommCard USA will supply your recording instructions

Step 3
Choose the amount of long distance calling time that you want activated on your cards. That's it.

Key Benefits:
- High profit margin
- Universally appealing, everyone can find value
- Keepsake (custom designed card image)
- Goodwill gesture as most will call their friends and family
- Continual promotional impact by using both the custom designed card image, and the custom audio message
- Excellent for sponsored or coop campaigns
- Unlimited creative opportunity
- Efficient, fits any budget
- Convenient and rewarding for all

For more information please contact
Rizzo & Associates
Paul C. Rizzo
262-248-0880

WAC
WESTERN ATHLETIC CONFERENCE

Boise State* • Fresno State • Hawaii
Louisiana Tech* • Nevada • Rice • San Jose State
SMU • TCU • UTEP • Tulsa

*WAC Member July, 2001

MEMO: December 18, 2000

TO: WAC HEAD BASKETBALL COACHES/STAFF (Men's & Women's) and
        BASKETBALL GAME MANAGEMENT PERSONNEL

FROM: Bill Foster, Special Asst. to the Commissioner of the
        WESTERN ATHLETIC CONFERENCE, Karl Benson

RE: Some Observations/Thoughts Regarding the Importance of Game
        Management for Basketball

Bill Foster (signature)

   I have appreciated talking to many personnel at each of our schools during my visits since the middle of October. Also, I have appreciated, at your games, your "attention to detail" regarding the very important role the management of the game plays in the success and reputation of our league.

   I feel that it's "preventive maintenance" of our great game. This coming season, I feel, upon seeing everyone practice and/or play in games, both men's and women's, that we will have a lot of very close contests. The atmosphere will build - emotions will be displayed - and competition will continue to build. It is my hope that your "attention to detail" will pay off so that we can prevent possible outbreaks/problems at any point of our games.

   From the time the first car pulls in to your parking lot or first person arrives at your arena, until the last fan leaves, "prevention" - security, and attention to detail -- all are extremely important. The management of the game; it involves so many people, from the mascot, to the cheerleaders, to the pep band, the parking personnel, campus and local police, food service/concessions, the "table people", the referees, emergency medical personnel, game security, ball boys/girls, ticket and marketing personnel, taking care of the media and their requests (if TV, another set of people to work with), the organization and planning of your entire operation, ready for any emergency; a broken rim, etc. - IT IS SO IMPORTANT -- few people are aware of the COMPLEXITY of this job -- and the RESPONSIBILITY.

   It is serious "stuff" - and I hope we're fortunate enough to have a terrific year in every way this coming season. It is also my hope that the WAC will be thought of again as a first-class league in every way - one that pays very close ATTENTION TO DETAIL and cares about the management of the game.

** BILL FOSTER, SPECIAL ASSISTANT TO THE COMMISSIONER OF THE WESTERN ATHLETIC CONFERENCE
   (WAC), KARL BENSON -- Mailing Address: PO Box 5295, Galveston, Texas 77554 ....
   PHONE: (409) 737-9470   ..... AND .....
   FAX: (409) 737-4856
   CELL: (409) 996-4545
                              9250 E. Costilla Ave., Suite 300
                              Englewood, CO 80112-3662
                              Phone: 303-799-9221   FAX: 303-799-3888
                              www.wacsports.com

MEMO to WAC Basketball Coaches/Game Managers (12/18/00)   Page Two
==

With that said - here are some of my personal comments about concerns that I have about every arena and every league -- with the additional comment that I am thankful that we have people at each of our schools that share this conern with me and it's much appreciated.

Some Additional "Specifics":

1. I do believe our game officials appreciate the security, protection, and hospitality they receive from their arrival at our arenas (special parking included) - your pre-game security, during and after each half, and to their end of game return to their parked vehicle. Also, the pre-game arrival of each school's "table people" to review any last minute thoughts/concerns PRIOR to the officials taking the floor - also most important. WAC HOSPITALITY is appreciated. Our officials, like most, work in different leagues and I hope they appreciate our league and our concern for security, hospitality, and safety.

   THE GAME MANAGER stopping by when the officials arrive, making sure they know who you are and where you will be sitting (most sit at the scorer's table at the end) is a big help. Same for those of you that are providing a post-game bag snack. This allows the game officials the luxury of NOT stopping by some place locally to get something to eat and come in contact with local fans and game attendees -- again, preventive maintenance.

   I also believe it's a good idea to greet the visiting head coach and his/her staff so they know who you are and can identify you & your role.

2. Some one in charge of ball boys/girls; important part of the game but sometime they need assistance and direction and reminders as the season rolls on (prevent slippage in this area). It's nice to see, in TV games, the ball boys/girls, ready and willing to help the officials take care of wet spots -- also to have on a distinctive (your university's name) and basketball t-shirt/sweat shirt.

   An area to watch for wet spots is the area near each team's bench on the quick time-outs with both teams not allowed to sit and they're actually on the playing floor (sideline).

3. Make sure various time-out and half-time programs on the playing floor are within the allowed time allotment.

THANKS VERY MUCH AND HAVE A TERRIFIC HOLIDAY.

Bill Foster

CHAPTER 9

USE OF DIRECT MAIL AND PERSONAL CONTACT — "GETTING THE WORD OUT"

This is another one of those chapters that an entire book could be written on each of the above topics instead of placing them all under Chapter Nine. Direct mail plays a very important role in sports marketing. One of the problems with this kind of mailing is the perception that it's junk mail.

Getting the person on the receiving end to OPEN THE ENVELOPE is a major part of the success of direct mail/marketing. When something comes from a coach, an athletic department, a recognizable person, a school, you've got a much higher percentage of success with that envelope being opened. It's important to have an attractive looking envelope, one that is easily identified, with the school's athletic department or coaching staff's return address on it. When it's recognizable, it will be opened just about 100% of the time.

The first thing of importance with direct mail is your mailing list. Is it accurate and up to date and is your list filled with a large number of names and addresses? The next important step is to TARGET your audience. You need to send to those that have some sort of interest, or connection, with your sports program or with the school. These are very important initial steps for success with direct mail. The cost involved with postage becomes a major item. First class mail, individually addressed, usually pulls a much better response percentage than any other. Special bulk mailings are much less expensive and might be worthwhile for special large general mailings. Of course, with this, you have to plan on a longer period of time for that mail to be received. You have to plan ahead and take into consideration that it will take longer and possibly be more perceived as junk mail. But you've got that all important return address that is recognizable. If you are going to spend the money for personalized first-class mail, you need to really TARGET your customers. You don't want to waste money on mail being undeliverable or going to people not interested in your school/program.

With a school, you have a great opportunity to not only TARGET your customers but also TO BUILD AN ACCURATE MAILING LIST. Some of the sources consist of: going through your alumni office and obtaining all the names of alumni that you might mail; you can definitely obtain a list of all the past letter winners; you have access to past season ticket holders; from the Chamber of Commerce you can get a list of area businesses and their owners/CEOs; names and addresses of the members of the student body and their parents, names and addresses of all the current members of all the athletic teams at the school; names and addresses of all of the faculty (in the case of the high school, make sure you have the junior high and elementary school faculty to send to); and you have those from the various booster clubs in your school, So this is a great start but that's only the beginning. You are ALWAYS BUILDING YOUR MAILING LIST. You now have online marketing with direct marketing done by e-mail and websites, which can be most effective and also less expensive. Everyone vitally involved with direct mail recommends that you TEST – TEST – TEST so that you get the most bang for your buck. Test the various methods you are using and also the costs involved with each in relation to the percentage of response and

> **With a school, you have a great opportunity to not only TARGET your customers but also TO BUILD AN ACCURATE MAILING LIST.**

> **You are ALWAYS BUILDING YOUR MAILING LIST.**

effectiveness. I believe you always "tweak" your methods to get maximum results. So direct e-mail programs are on the rise.

E-mail is a very good medium to reach customers. It's fast, cheap and generally has a very good response rate. It's particularly good IF they are already your customers. If not, they can delete your name in a hurry. If you have the "name recognition", you've got a better chance for a response. E-mail marketing requires creative promos to get attention. This method might be utilized to attract a larger crowd, with SPECIAL PRICE TICKETING for exhibition games that don't sell out.

> **I believe an important part of your direct marketing in athletics can be the NEWSLETTER.**

I believe an important part of your direct marketing in athletics can be the NEWSLETTER. This is a very effective method to not only "get the word out" but also give your preferred fans some "inside scoop" on their team(s). Newsletters have to be informative and provide RECENT news. It helps in athletics to have basically an "all good news" publication. With the computer and computer art, you can easily design and product a first class attractive piece. Don't forget you should touch the recent and the past with this. I've always liked a "What They Are Doing NOW" section as people always want to know what their past players are doing today. In another chapter, we mention providing specific content that attracts and keeps attention —pictures are always popular. YOU are the producer, so make it "good news" and SELL – SELL – SELL. There should be a feature on the front page advertising the UPCOMING DATES/EVENTS so your subscribers/customers/fans can make their plans in advance.

I prefer to see a strong sales letter going along with the season ticket flyer. You can personalize it much better. I'm amazed at how many schools just stick the season ticket brochure in an envelope along with a pocket schedule and ship it out.

If you have a short and timely message to get out that doesn't necessarily have to be in an envelope, I like the over-sized postcard. Check with the postal authorities on how large you can go for the least expense. This method can get your message across quickly (you don't have to get it out of an envelope), it can be eye-catching, and the postage expense is much less.

The person I have referred to many times as one of the best, if not the best in direct marketing, DAN KENNEDY, likes to use what he calls "grabbers"; they grab your attention. These "grabbers" can consist of an actual penny, dollar bill, one of those fake million dollar bills, sample packs of aspirin, or Tylenol, etc. Thinking of the latter two (aspirin and Tylenol), wouldn't that be a creative marketer's dream sending out news on the upcoming season? Something like, "You Won't Need Tylenol This Coming

I prefer to see a strong sales letter going along with the season ticket flyer.

Season As This Team Won't Give You A Headache", or plenty of other "plays" on this insert. It does get your attention.

On your original letter to purchase tickets and attend games, if you have a powerful person endorsing the upcoming exciting season – that can be a plus. In most cases, it's the coach with his comments and this works fine. Put a lot of thought into this.

Throughout various chapters in this book, we've touched upon the importance of personal contact. This can be through your personal contact with fans, the coaching staff, the mascot and cheerleaders, and anyone directly related to the program. It's important that someone is setting up those speaking engagements either at Rotary, dormitories, fraternities, sororities, or in a mall. The more you have your people OUT AND ABOUT, the more popular they generally become. Some of your people might have to be prompted. You may want to provide a "script" of ideas that will help YOU sell the team a little bit easier. Players could be called upon also. I've mentioned that the use of the mascot can be powerful. I think baseball teams have done a great job of promoting and utilizing their mascots. Many of the colleges and universities will "tour the state" in the spring – usually with their football and basketball coach. This is a popular function, particularly with their alumni groups. Sometimes they become the "off Broadway" production

> **The more you have your people OUT AND ABOUT, the more popular they generally become.**

of "Promises – Promises" but they work. You want to get visibility for your head coach and your team. While you're at it, work at getting the young kids involved with coming to the games. Many school's have a special section/ticket prices and a club-type operation that works. Start them young and you've got many years of their being a good fan. Those players are role-models whether they want to be or not. This is another advantage for the colleges and the high schools.

GETTING THE WORD OUT . . . and inexpensively too.

You have to love the challenge. Exciting; every day different and you get to visit with lots of people. Plus that SCOREBOARD, measuring this year's attendance vs. last year, showing progress, is the envy of others. It's a real MOTIVATOR for you and your staff. Being able to MEASURE RESULTS is something others can't do except the coaches with their won-loss record. You get to work with players and coaches from your school and with the competition. You have an opportunity to meet those from your opponent. What a great way to enjoy what you are doing, to network, and demonstrate your skills.

We're going to list many ideas for you to "GET THE WORD OUT" about your team(s) either free, inexpensive, or possibly by "co-op"

> **You want to get visibility for your head coach and your team.**

> **Being able to MEASURE RESULTS is something others can't do except the coaches with their won-loss record.**

arrangement. Be an "ACTION" person.

1. Local Walk-A-Thon placing flyers with a rubber band around the doorknob of each home. We're seeing more and more of this especially with pizza companies with their special offers and coupons. Carefully pre-plan the walking routes and assign different streets. It's not a bad idea to have teams of two people doing this for safety.

2. Placing pocket schedules and season ticket information at restaurants. Fast food businesses will usually allow you to put information on their counters. It's good to use cardboard holders so your flyers will stay organized. You might be able to talk them in to handing out with each "drive through" order also.

    The same for grocery stores, usually they are willing to allow their check-out people to insert your material into each sack.

3. At large and well attended events, with all those cars in a parking lot, place your flyers or information under the windshield wiper of each car. Two problems with this would be rain/snow while the car sits in the lot, AND the fact that a lot of them will be thrown away on the parking lot instead of placed IN their car (not a good way to gain friends).

4. Conduct a coaching clinic. Get a "big-name" speaker who will not only attract a good crowd but will ENDORSE your team/program. Make sure you have media in attendance with a photographer and video person.

> **Make sure you have media in attendance with a photographer and video person.**

5. If local monthly statements are coming from a bank or other business by mail, ask to have your small "filler" go in with the mailing; no additional cost to the business (all for one ounce). You'll probably need a "fan friendly" executive at their end to approve this.

6. Conduct camp/clinics for kids – free if possible, but as in every other promotion you have, get those names, mailing addresses, e-mail information, and phone numbers, of all in attendance. To get this, you might have each attendee fill out a printed card and drop in a box for a special drawing for door prizes. You should always be working to BUILD YOUR MAILING LIST and these would be excellent because they've already attended an event at your school or on your campus. You might want to put a place for "Parent's Name" on that form also because they might be a prospective season-ticket buyer.

7. If you have that "Special Committee of 100" or whatever number you might be able to put together, ASK EACH to get you the names

and addresses of FIVE MORE people to help you BUILD YOUR MAILING LIST. This can help you build that list in a hurry.

8. Work out any arrangement with a printer to "trade-out" printing costs for tickets/good seats to your events. Posters with schedules on them are popular but expensive and this might be a good way to get these free – or you can have a business sponsor with their advertising on it.

9. We've already mentioned NEWSLETTERS either by direct mail or by e-mail and possibly both.

10. Theatres – special ads on the screen prior to the feature movie. Movie attendance has been on the upswing. Expense might be taken care of by way of trade-out.

11. "Take to your Neighbor" campaign – each student at school take two/four of your flyers, or whatever, home and give one to each neighbor next door and maybe one or two directly across the street. Size of student body or group involved, determines the number of "potential hits".

12. Special group, like girl scouts, boy scouts, special interest group; take home flyers for their parents and next-door neighbors. You could

trade-out tickets and get more of these young people to attend your event.

13. One big campaign – possibly pre-season, delivering the sports schedules for the entire season, or a packet of information; have each parent take to their place of employment and make available to their co-workers. This might not give the geographical area you want BUT you're getting the MESSAGE OUT to a lot of people. There may be some duplication on this but no problem.

14. Hand-outs to students during classes or an assembly program.

15. Attend service club (Rotary, Lions, etc.) and/or Chamber of Commerce meetings and hand out flyers/schedule. Better yet, do this with your coach being the main speaker and him making a personal appeal to come out and see "YOUR HOME TOWN'" team play.

16. Advertise "special nights" like "Jam The Gym Night" to set an attendance record – "be a part of this record-setting event".

17. Schedule pre-season breakfast or special fan get-together/autographs, etc. and possibly involve a local celebrity.

18. Sponsor any kind of popular event with your team to get people to attend; for example, pre-season basketball night (midnight madness), with both men's and women's teams; or possibly combine with a

faculty game or alumni night. Add to this "Meet and Greet The Team" with autographs and picture taking.

19. A special game; exhibition, scrimmage or intra-squad, conducted by and for a local worthy and popular charity. They would publicize (work with them carefully on this – they may NOT be as experienced at this as you are) and basically sell the seats (or donation). This would bring in "new" fans to your arena/stadium (again, try to get the names and addresses for your mailing list).

<u>EXPOSURE — EXPOSURE — EXPOSURE</u>

<u>SELL — SELL — SELL</u>

Let's pause here for a minute. Three Important Thoughts:

a. Think and analyze — will it be successful (if not, don't do it).

b. With the above — "plan for successful events/promotions only".

c. Do we have the time and staff to market properly?

AGAIN, plan only for successful promotions – think it through clearly; meet with your staff, brainstorm, and then make your "educated" guess on what will probably work and what won't.

20. For building your fan base; produce a printed form with ten blanks on it with space for the name and mailing address (for ten different

AGAIN, plan only for successful promotions

people). If they are properly filled out and returned to you with all ten, you send them a free t-shirt (make sure you list approximate size on your form) – or other appropriate item with a "perceived" value. This could be your school's logo'd t-shirt or whatever. We did this for years for our basketball camp and it was tremendously successful for building our mailing list. Make those cards post-paid postcards to be returned to you.

21. I've always liked to have a light cardboard stock, one panel (one third of an 8- x 11" paper) that FITS into a NUMBER TEN ENVELOPE with attractively printed information on an upcoming event OR info just selling your program. You would have this available for every secretary or administrative person in your school to enclose and send out with every piece of mail that is being sent. This is a "filler" and needs no additional postage.

22. If the coach or anyone connected with the school is involved with a radio or TV show — make sure you have some "free spots" ready to sell your product.

23. If your coach has a radio or TV show; prepare a small flyer with his/her picture on it, show the station and time, and any other pertinent information. Prepare this as a "filler" to also have your staff send out

with any and all mailings that won't require additional postage. This can be on 8.5 by 11" paper. Make it attractive to help SELL the show and in return, they'll help you sell events.

24. "CREATE" a news release — work on a unique news story surrounding your team, coach or player(s) or any circumstance that is unusual and might attract attention. You would put this out as a Press Release. Design an attractive logo/letterhead with "Special News Coming From: (your name)". Make sure you also have your phone/fax/e-mail information on it as well as your mailing address.

25. "GET THE ENTIRE FAMILY OUT" night/day; work on some game/event that the entire family can attend as a group and sit together with neighbors and friends. This gets "numbers" in the seats and creates interest. It's a "special" way to attend a game. Remember the drive-in movies where it was one price per carload.

The Texas Rangers baseball team has several special nights consisting of a $9.00 ticket (upper deck) with the entire group together. That ticket price also includes a hot dog and a drink. Other teams have special bleacher seats with a reduced cost. The Chicago Cubs have been doing a terrific job with this.

26. Anything going out to your fans/season ticket holders, and the like; getting decals out or key chains with the name of the team on it as well as printed merchandise like t-shirts, are all well received. Those attractively printed t-shirts with the team's logo, etc., are very popular.

27. Community Bulletin Boards. Many areas have these boards where you can place current information and items on upcoming events. Many are in the lobby of local YMCAs, churches, libraries, senior centers and civic centers.

28. Your newsletter should go on your WEB SITE – add to it, keep fresh and informative material on it.

29. If you have a college team — using computer art, make up a practice schedule for your team, including a letter from the head coach, and INVITE ENTIRE HIGH SCHOOL AND/OR JUNIOR HIGH SCHOOL TEAMS TO ATTEND ONE OF YOUR ACTUAL PRACTICE SESSIONS. Actually, this can be useful to high schools by inviting junior highs and possibly elementary school teams and their coaches to the practice. You'll list the days and the time of practice on this. All a junior high or high school coach has to do is call in to the listed telephone number and ask for a certain coach

(listed on the flyer) and tell them what date you will be attending. Now at the actual practice session, make sure you have a manager ready to meet and greet the group and give each a copy of that day's practice schedule, game schedules, roster of the players with numbers, etc. – also get those names and addresses of each attendee. We have a copy of that flyer/invitation in this book for your use. This is also a terrific public relations device which can be quite popular. (see two-page example in Chapter Eleven).

30. CREATE an assembly program that you can take around to your junior high schools, or if a college, to high schools. Take two or three of your athletes with you to be involved in your question and answer session. You can "script" the questions. The athletes are excellent advertisements for your program. You would take ticket information schedules, posters, and the like, along with you to have handed out to each attending student. Make it entertaining and as quick hitting as you possibly can. If you can take along your MASCOT, this helps to "lighten" up the program. Have a recording of your fight song for effect and it can be a fun program. Make sure it's not more than about 45 minutes in length.

Years ago, in basketball, when I was at the University of Utah, we did a "Challenge the Utes" assembly program primarily for junior high schools. It consisted of showing our highlights film. We did a short question and answer program with our two attending players. We had the school furnish us with 10 to 15 questions on 3x5 cards and the players had an opportunity to look at these ahead of time. We had to borrow a pick-up truck to transport the portable backboard. The school would pick out one boy and one girl to compete in the free-throw shooting contest in front of the entire student body at the assembly program. Now that's pressure. The contest involved a "best of ten" shots to determine the winner of this challenge. If a college, and you have a short recruiting video, this would be excellent. Actually, my first year at Duke University, we also used this and called it, "Challenge the Blue Devils". Schools are always looking to pick up different types of assembly programs so we had an easy time of setting these up.

31. Any game that is fully sponsored by a business should make sure the business supports it with print advertising. For example, any tie in with, say, MacDonalds , you could get two free tickets to your exhibition game on Saturday night IF you bought a Big Mac, fries,

and a beverage. As part of our agreement, sell them a large number of tickets at a low price per ticket but make sure your agreement includes their advertising in the local paper listing the game and details. I believe this is an excellent way to get more attendees at exhibition games — those games that don't draw as well.

32. Your BOOSTER CLUB MEMBERS can get to other people thru next door neighbors, or various clubs and groups (women's bridge groups, church groups, seniors, etc.) about anything you need to get out.

33. Create an INFORMATION TABLE of current events available at each of your home games. Use a strategic location (or two) for this set-up. At events where you have ticket takers, have them hand out important information or UTILIZE YOUR VOLUNTEERS in this way.

On your table, be sure to keep things neat and in an orderly fashion and replenish as needed. Have a person designated to be responsible for this. This table can include "special" up to date game promos, summer camp information, upcoming games, clinics, etc. MAKE USE OF THIS FREE OPPORTUNITY.

34. On your FAX COVER SHEET – take advantage of all that space available TO SELL. You can put your remaining schedule on it (along the side) keep up to date with only the remaining games.

35. Develop a monthly sporting event calendar – you'll note that in many newspapers with all the sports they have to cover, they will do one with the upcoming week. These can be sent out as "fillers" or placed in strategic places to be picked up.

36. Another idea which I don't particularly like, at busy intersections with traffic lights, on the "red" stop, you can hand out pertinent information. You would probably have to check with the police and traffic department, to get approval for this.

37. TRADE-OUTS can get excellent free exposure – particularly true with radio shows (sports talk shows), and newspapers. Exchange for free tickets.

38. DON'T FORGET YOUR FACULTY AND STAFF. The more faculty you can get interested and attending, the better it becomes. Have a "faculty only" practice with beverage and cookies at the end. They get to watch a practice and of course, those managers hand them all the background info like roster with numbers, etc. Don't be disappointed with small numbers at first, but like everything you are

doing, work to BUILD it. Make sure your faculty is on your mailing list. ALSO, some schools do a great job of having a different faculty member as an honorary assistant coach and sit on the bench. They are introduced as part of the pre-game introductions also. This is an excellent public relations gesture.

39. I like the idea of each coach of the teams that you are marketing; prepare a small "fundamentals of the game" notebook, with an attractive cover (computer art), to use for kids and fans available free. This can be prepared on the computer and possibly sent out with season tickets, etc. For basketball, just a fundamentals of shooting pamphlet would be a valuable "gift" item.

40. For extra publicity, you can always use a "Mayor's Challenge" or a celebrity cha11enge a few days before game time. This sparks more interest and definitely gains you more media coverage and attention. You can have some type of "CUP'" (rotating) to the winner.

41. If your games are on radio, thoroughly "brief" your announcing team. They need to help you SELL, SELL, SELL and can be a great boost to you. The same for any pre or post-game coaches shows and the same for TV games. If you have both radio and TV, check to see if you are getting the most sales push that you can possibly get.

Anytime I think of communications, announcing teams and excitement for games, I think of DICK VITALE AND COLLEGE BASKETBALL. I have heard Dick do many games, have had him do our games, and also had DICK VITALE NIGHT as a pre-season "fan night" and its always his enthusiasm that is contagious as well as an upbeat personality that you get every night.

42. Colleges/high schools: Take advantage of HOMECOMING celebrations; great opportunity to enlist alums and CULTIVATE THAT MAILING LIST.

43. "Signage" anywhere close to the event can be very helpful. If your school has their own electronic or manual sign spots, use them and keep up to date. Stringing a large sign across the street telling of an upcoming game, can't be too expensive. Again, the trade-out route might be best for this.

I recently passed a sign in front of a Baptist Church in Jamaica Beach (Texas), it said: "Pastor said we should change this message, so I did". Lots of people have commented on this and now take a closer look at their sign to see what's up there.

FREE PUBLICITY should be a KEY COMPONENT OF YOUR MARKETING STRATEGY. You need to actively cultivate the news media. You should have periodic get-togethers with the media and your coaches with refreshments. Remember, they have only so much space to work with and more and more local and national sports to cover. Develop a terrific relationship with everyone of them.

TEN MOST IMPORTANT WORDS:

"If It Is To Be —Then It's Up To Me"

I liked the cartoon with the guy looking up at the street sign saying, "EASY STREET" and the road blocked off with a sign, "CLOSED FOR REPAIRS".

CHAPTER 10

FILLING SEATS FIRST —
NEXT STEP IS SELLING SEATS,
INCLUDING PRICING

You and your school must have some sort of philosophy and plan on how the climate is for "give-away" seats. Everyone wants to sell seats but if you are involved in a program that is "down" and is not rich in tradition and possibly with a small enrollment, give-aways will be tough. Your philosophy still is to BUILD ONE FAN AT A TIME. You don't have a lot of time but you've got to get a cooperative effort between the school's administration, the coaching staff and yourself. You can't bring this to life immediately without

> **The players have to adopt a most positive attitude and express this new attitude when talking with friends and strangers.**

everyone pitching in and doing their part. In fact, the coach has to get the players to "sign off" on the game plan for resurrecting the program. The players have to adopt a most positive attitude and express this new attitude when talking with friends and strangers. The school has to show support toward this change in attitude and in confidence that things will get better and then you still better pray a lot. You also need luck on your side. In these types of situations, teams are lacking in quality of depth and any - injury will prove to be a major setback.

So, you have your hands full. You keep positive; very positive and plow ahead. You just roll up your sleeves and plan, work, organize, build, and keep moving forward.

For others, their school has a pretty good team and few people show up for games. Dig around to get at the bottom of this. There will be a lot of reasons and you have to work at building the same way – one fan at a time. You'll probably have to have a lot of give-aways but somehow you've got to work at getting money to come in to support the program. The old problem of not wanting to cheapen the season ticket by giving seats away crops up and is real. You may start under the guise of charity or helping the youth groups, or seniors. But if you do, make sure their seats, if they are give-aways, aren't better than the season ticket holder. You can sell those season tickets by first, informing all who will listen, that those 50-yard line, "oceanfront" seats are available and will be going on a first served basis. Stress how they'll be on the ground floor of a program that will be turning it around soon and that seats will be hard to come by in the future – especially good seats like those available now. Also, you target businesses using the same approach. They don't want to be left out and if they buy NOW, they've got a chance to buy great seats. Save your give-aways until last and then you go for the boy and girl scouts, and other groups including church groups and various civic groups. We discuss in other sections of the book about various plans to sell and to give-away. You first need to organize a group to help you sell. People who will make phone calls to friends and neighbors and directly ask them for their support – buy tickets. Start first with season tickets – the full package. Now your creative mind comes up with a "three-pack" – pick any three games and have good seats but not the best. Or pick any number depending on the sport – you need to not only be creative but ready to wheel and deal. You don't want to change prices once they are set but you don't want to lose a customer. Originally, you should make sure your product is not over-priced. If you have a bad situation and trying to improve, it's better to under-price than to over-price.

Tight fiscal control is a must.

Again, have help with your sales. Get more people involved and have them prepared with a sales pitch that you have "scripted". Set up phone-a-thons and have the coaching staff involved making calls. You'll be spending some money but you want to make hard decisions what you can spend on and how much. Tight fiscal control is a must. In this situation, you'll find it's much easier to spend money than to make money. Again, make your pricing attractive to the customer under these tough circumstances. Initially, when you are selling (and always have on hand a seating chart of your stadium and arena), you'll be able to point out specifically exactly where their seats will be. Also, they are told that next year, they'll have the option to have those same great seats again. They'll build friendships with the people around them and that helps with the renewals. If they have an objection on price, you can show them the exact location of the next least expensive seating. And, in your pricing you can go down to your seats farthest from the action, maybe you'll have a $2.00 seat available. So you give them the option. Your next objection will be, we won't be able to go to every game. We're working, both of us, etc. Then you meet this objection head on —you tell them they want to keep those great seats, and the few games they will miss they can give to "make a new fan" of a neighbor. Or, they can sell those on their own, because they are such great seats. People want prime seating and you should do everything you can to make those people comfortable and have a perk or two or three. They came up with the money and bought early and got you started. You don't want to lose those folks.

With your second year on the job, you'll be better acquainted with the landscape and you'll not only know the area/situation better but you'll also have a better plan and team to sell more seats. You'll be able to implement – more ideas and not "spin you wheels" as much as that first year.

For those that have been in marketing at their school, much the same is part of your blueprint to sell more, much more, that you did a year ago. Select those ideas that you feel will work. Make sure they fit into the time frame that you and your staff have and roll up those sleeves. Take your ideas and write them down in the order of your priority, your priority being those that you feel will work the best and the fastest. While you are doing this, you might want to implement your staff with more "student interns" for your sports marketing team. Make sure you have the workspace, the job description, the available good personnel, and get started on developing and building your team.

When you start out with your PRICING – keep in mind several definites. If the price is too high, you'll get objections galore, and if it's too low you'll catch grief from up above. You have to research your pricing structure right from the start. What was last year's pricing schedule. What will the traffic bear? Can we price it a little lower and sell more seats? What is the structure of our neighboring schools? You can justify prices easier if they correspond to some degree with the other schools in your league.

Make sure you are getting top dollar for those GREAT seats. Then scale it down correspondingly. You know that by far the most difficult will be to sell the ones farthest away. Don't be afraid to create those top row seats at a really reduced price – remember, they buy at the concessions stand too and that will add up. Also, on pricing, take into consideration the strength and popularity of your team – particularly for the upcoming season. You do have to consider the problem you will have with those in the top row leaving their seats and filling in down below. You've got to weigh all factors and come with an "educated guess" – and you can test things out with your advisory board. You'll have to run your price structure by your immediate boss to get his/her approval – A MUST.

As you survey your entire athletic program and you find that you have a sport that you did NOT charge admission, and NOW, you feel you should, this requires some serious thinking. Pricing becomes an issue and can be a delicate situation. People used to getting in free will now have to pay. You must get the word out to all as to what you are doing and WHY. Rather than go with a very low single game ticket price, as well as a low priced season ticket (remember you'll need ticket sellers and takers/staff), you might want to go with a one price season ticket for preferred seats like $20 for the season.

By the way, in areas that have a lot of building of new homes, YOU should be the local "welcome wagon" – get in there first with your sales pitch and a small basket of fruit. Try to get them committed and involved and make new friends. Those pre- and post-game socials really help those that are new in the community.

While we're involved with the pricing structure of your job, it's important that we look at some other prerequisites for doing a great job in sports marketing to be successful:

- ** Effective leadership
- ** Being able to get along with others (people skills), and enjoying your work.
- ** Ability to get others involved including campus community as well as students, boosters and your community (town & gown).
- ** And probably most importantly, getting along with the coaches and athletes themselves.

> ** Your superiors/administrators and you must work within the framework and philosophy of your school and still be able to build an <u>aggressive marketing program.</u>

SOME MISCELLANEOUS BUT IMPORTANT CONSIDERATIONS REGARDING YOUR PRICING AND YOUR SALES PLAN:

1. Any ticket sales you set up should be easy and efficient for the buyer. During the last football season, I just picked up the phone and called three different high schools in three different states. I had the phone number of the athletic department only. I called to get a schedule and to find out the cost of season tickets. It took me forever to get this information — I know that in mid-August, you might not be fully staffed BUT, it's the beginning of football season. CHECK TO DETERMINE HOW DIFFICULT THIS IS AT YOUR SCHOOL and check from time to time. This is where an advisory board could be helpful in making sure the "little things" are fan friendly – although this is NOT a little thing. You can't allow anything dealing with the customer or potential customer to "slip through the cracks".

2. On your ticket sales; and in particular, season ticket sales, determine what the major objections are? Make sure your ticket personnel write

You can't allow anything dealing with the customer or potential customer to "slip through the cracks".

down ALL objections and log them for you. They are on the "front line" and will hear problems, probably more than you, so ENCOURAGE them to write them down and get them to you quickly. Solving those problems immediately is important – as important as getting a nice letter back to the person who called in with the complaint. Taking care of that with a personal follow-up letter, and quickly, will be a "shock" to most people, It's done less and less today.

3. A tried and true formula for getting more people into the seats for a football game is to have band night/day competition. It might even work in basketball but I think it would be too much noise in an enclosed arena.

4. The top two objections to season ticket sales in the pros apparently are No. 1 – cost; and #2 – too many games (both may work, we can't attend all), in no particular order

    One way to meet the #2 objection above is to have the head coach write to every season ticket holder (excellent for high school and most colleges), and first, THANK THEM for buying the tickets. Then explain that IF they can't make every game, that they should give them to a friend who will attend and cheer for the Wildcats (you're always looking to add new fans). Of course, some may be sold but encourage them to have local fans attend. This way you have more home team fans in the stands, less empty seats, and more sales at the concession stand. In basketball, it's best to have a letter from the coach sent right before that first exhibition game. You want to encourage them to attend that game and the need to have them in attendance to cheer for the team, you can talk about the opponent's strengths and of course, they'll have a good chance to see the new players, etc. Then send another letter around January 1st as you get into league play reminding them of the same.

5. To meet objection #1 above – cost – make attractive lesser number of games ticket packages, hopefully you can offer good seats. Of course, their seats will not be quite as good as the full season ticket holders who get first choice.

6. Market your area hard. Determine the geographic area you can effectively market and cover it well. Experiment with expanding it a little at a time.

7. "Specials" always get attention. Do some kind of "special" with your Spring Football game and your basketball exhibition game. Also, have another "hook" to get people to those games. I really admire those

schools that have such a great demand that their football and basketball exhibition games are sold out.

8. Along with the pricing of tickets, you have ticket pick-up and the potential for long lines at popular games. We're seeing now with expanding technology, different and easier methods of not only purchasing tickets but also delivery. Ticketmaster offers the purchase of tickets over the INTERNET and payment along with a printed ticket available through your own printer. People with Ticketmaster are saying that they see the day when you don't even have to bring in your ticket; you download the information into your cell phone and bring that with you (doesn't everybody?). They then scan your phone when you enter the event. Now for the rest of the story; there has to be some cost. We're hearing that it's only an extra dollar. Prior, apparently with Federal Express delivery, the cost was higher.

9. Target your audience; cater to kids, families, students, seniors, and the businesses. Make sure you have them all on your mailing list. For half-time shows, when you book a large group of kids to appear and perform, make sure you have a very special price, if any, for their parents. Try to get them to stay for the second half (maybe a special

drawing for door prizes). How about the concessions on those nights; do kids eat? Wow!

10. Target getting those "Special Days/Nights" and have them sponsored by a business. They get a large number of tickets for a special price. They bring a lot of people. Have them sitting together and throw in perks like special parking passes.

11. In your direct marketing of tickets, it's more than a "one-shot" effort to be most effective. It should be designed to have a SEQUENCE OF FOLLOW-UPS to improve your percentage of response. A good way to follow up that first letter with a minimum of work, is to take the original letter and just put one of those large yellow "post-up" sheets on the top of the first page with a handwritten short message like, "In case you didn't receive our original letter, we're sending it again, we need YOU with US".

12. Factor in everything you can when you come up with your group rates. You can set a number for groups from 10 to 20; 21 to 30, etc. You will target businesses, church groups, service club groups, school groups (student prices go into this also), charitable organizations, and the like. You also factor in the price for the very large groups like

"IBM Night", and those types whereby the business or organization has the "naming" rights to that event.

13. If you have telephone sales, make sure they are well prepared to take the orders, anticipate questions, and can make it a smooth transaction. Sometimes these people are the only "contact" an outsider may have with the school and the athletic program, so it makes it so important that you have "fan friendly" people who are courteous and helpful manning the phones. Put a smile in that voice.

> **Put a smile in that voice.**

14. Try to personalize as much as possible, whether it be order taking or everything involved with the game – people are becoming more and more irritated over the "lack" of personalization and inability to speak to someone instead of recorded messages.

15. Timing is so important in advance sales. Plus, advance sales are so important to the overall success of your ticket selling program. Sell when you're undefeated is the best time to sell. You want to get that money in early, however you need the interest in the team necessary to make that sale. Decisions – Decisions – Decisions. You have to make everything sound exciting and get the fan interested ahead of time. And by the way, make that order form simple. Clearly outline the BENEFITS to the season ticket holder to purchase early.

16. You work twelve months out of the year to obtain corporate sponsors. You've got everything available and have a clear pricing plan. You've got signage, title sponsor for games, large group special seating and pricing, work on corporate outings, all sorts of sponsorships including radio, TV, half-time shows, scoreboard, scorer's table, time-out programs, etc. Any more, people put a dollar figure on anything that is stationary or movable – that means practically everything – and they usually get it so why not you? Don't be afraid to throw in a perk or two on the larger dollar items. If you have free parking, add a "Preferred Location" and add several of these as incentives. People like special attention and preferred status.

17. Aggressively pursue radio and TV opportunities. Be creative in your approach and offer benefits to the stations and the sponsors. Put all these potential opportunities on your mailing list – not only for ticket information, but also for any flyers, brochures, and newsletters.

18. And … don't forget CUSTOMER SERVICE… all thriving businesses have made this a PRIORITY… and so must you. Constant meetings with all of your personnel who work closely with the PUBLIC, stressing the importance of being friendly and helpful is a must. Also, stressing to your workers on how important each of them are to the

overall success of your operation. You might want to appoint a "Director of Good Will" to check and double- check on this important phase of your work. We have provided information previously in this book on the importance of game management (Chapter Eight).

19. If you can create a "fun" atmosphere at your games, this can be very important, especially if you will be drawing a lot of kids. Your MASCOT can be highly involved in this. The atmosphere can be created inside your arena/stadium or outside. I won't forget attending the first WNBA game in Los Angeles. It was the New York Liberty at the Los Angeles Sparks. Coming in to the arena it was a carnival atmosphere. They had elaborate pre-game festivities as well as post-game and it was terrific. The NBA and the WNBA do a terrific job of marketing their product. You want to watch what they are doing closely and get some ideas from them.

20. On pricing, you might want to have a special price for visiting teams to help build your attendance. You could get in touch with the other team's representative prior to the season, and determine whether they might want to have a special "alumni or fan-type" night when they come to play you on your home court. For a college, it would be a

good idea to contact your opponent's alumni office. In the Western Athletic Conference, you might have a San Jose State or Hawaii or any of our teams coming in for a league game at Rice University (Houston), those schools might want to schedule an alumni get-together or fan meeting prior to the game with all of their Houston area fans/alums. I think this makes a lot of sense but it does require a lot of work. You would have to reserve a special block of seats, somewhere fairly near the opponent's bench to add to the festivities. This idea can add more fans in the seats (paying fans even though it would be a special price), good public relations for your school, their group cheering for their team and this would bring a more exciting atmosphere to the home team's stadium/arena. This could also be accomplished with high school teams. When you have fans cheering from both sides, this really adds to the high school/college atmosphere. At pro games, usually you have most everyone cheering for the home team – it's more one-sided.

21. Although it's not involved with pricing, if you do happen to be on TV you need to really work at having a full house. TV games with half- full stadiums/arenas don't exactly show off your school in a good way. It shows that there's not quite the interest nor the enthusiasm for

your team. Work to even "stage" that TV event – YOU are the producer. Signs, organized cheering, and overall, putting on a real show for the viewers really HELPS THE IMAGE AND PERCEPTION OF YOUR SCHOOL. Everyone wants to be on TV, but it may not prove to be good if your school/team doesn't come across well on that tube.

22. In your pricing structure, you have to constantly remind yourself and your other decision makers, that you are in STRICT COMPETITION FOR THE SPORTS AND ENTERTAINMENT DOLLAR. One of the big problems today with attendance is the FACT that not only is there more going on, with better coverage, more TV and radio, but also the professional teams have much larger budgets to make attractive flyers and buy promotion and marketing opportunities with the media. I might add that they usually have a much larger staff. THIS IS WHY YOUR ABILITY TO ALSO DO SOME FUND RAISING TO GET MORE MONEY IN YOUR BUDGET FOR MARKETING IS A PRIORITY .

Your motto will probably be: "Nobody ever said it was going to be easy".

No one stands pat anymore. They can't afford to. Some team(s) will be gaining on you. There is just more of everything today compared to ten, fifteen, twenty years ago. There are more sports, different sports, more pro teams, more theatres, more vacation attractions, more health clubs, better and more expensive advertising, more experts in the marketing of teams/events, more concerts, and so YOU ARE IN A RACE.

Teams look to the corporate world to bail them out but this can't do it alone. Season ticket sales are the best and most predictable method to sell your seats. But, you must fill those seats out with single game sales plus those special days/nights. "WINNING CURES A LOT OF ILLS" and so does it help to have an EXCITING AND HUSTLING TEAM. It also helps to be trying to sell a sport in an area where that sport is very popular. Texas high school football is legendary. Soccer is more popular in Hispanic communities. Baseball usually works a little better in warm-weather climate. But just as important, are your STUDENTS. They lend a real degree of ENTHUSIASM and EXCITEMENT and SPONTANEITY to your game. Add the cheerleaders, the band and your mascot and special student cheering sections, you've got it going. I've always said when I was coaching basketball, that I never wanted to start a game without the pep band, and I meant It. Add all this together plus increasing the noise level adds up to a nice home-field/court advantage which helps the players and the coaches.

23. In the "off season" for your sport(s), write to other schools to get their season ticket flyers, brochures, press guides and the like. Samples of what others are doing can be helpful to you in the future. Always have a folder in your brief case, titled: "IDEAS FOR NEXT YEAR", and just keep putting ideas that come to your mind, or you see, in that folder for the future. It's also a good idea to pick out several pro teams and write them and establish contact and get their material.

> **Always have a folder in your brief case, titled: "IDEAS FOR NEXT YEAR", and just keep putting ideas that come to your mind, or you see, in that folder for the future.**

24. Your challenge will be to sell those "mountain view" seats and the last rows. I'm sure you'll have dreams about having a "full house". I loved the author/marketing expert, Jon Spoelstra's (see back of book for specifics) description of "beach-front property" and the "mountain view" seats – that says it all. Special selling points have to be CREATED to sell those less desirable seats. In football, "get closer to the scoring" goes along with selling end zone seats. Your challenge also might be selling those bleacher seats. Perhaps an excellent give-away for you would be those portable padded seat cushions — you

> **Special selling points have to be CREATED to sell those less desirable seats.**

can bring them to the game and take them home with you. Bleacher seats are a tougher sell and you should make every attempt to add more and more chairbacks... much more comfortable.

25. You are in the business of making money. Investigating all possibilities is most important. The idea of "packaging" has been a concept that has become more and more popular. Instead of expenses all being placed in your hands, it's shared with another either business or school.

One way to increase sales would be to "assess" your upcoming schedule. Are there two or three games that definitely will not "draw" fans too well? If so, you can offer the boy or girl scouts or some service group, an OPPORTUNITY to make money without any risk. If your seats were selling for $8.00 per seat, you would give these seats (a particular number) on consignment to the scouts, let's say, and they would only have to pay half price for them when they're sold at $4.00. Thus they could make a nice amount of money. It's particularly inviting with larger groups like the band. It's a "win-win" situation — they sell the seats for you, they make money, and you'll have more people in the stands. You need to have someone assigned to keep on top of these groups. You just can't hand them out and forget. Call and check on how things are going. Do they need more tickets? You can offer this opportunity to any high school or college group that needs to raise money, as well as church groups.

26. I've already mentioned adding more front row seats and given some examples of what you can do and what price you might charge. SMU a year ago was able to add 32 courtside seats at a cost of $30 per game, per seat, and they quickly sold out for the basketball season. If my math serves me correctly, that's an additional $14,400 total income over a fifteen game home stand. That's being creative and resourceful.

27. I've always felt the "social" aspect of the tail-gating at football games has been a big selling point. These are both pre-game and post-game. How about trying to initiate this for basketball? I'm sure there are a few schools in the warmer climates attempting this. I hope it's successful. You'd have to build this concept as thus far, it's been a Fall activity and not one for the Winter. Of course, with baseball, it's more of a natural. When this becomes a big social event, families PLAN years in advance to get together.

28. To go along with your marketing and creating an atmosphere that you are "fan friendly" and appreciate your fans – schedule a "Fan

Appreciation Day/Night" at least once a year. This should be promoted as a big deal with give-ways and drawings for valuable prizes. These prizes would all be donated. It's a nice way to say "thank you" to the people who are keeping you going.

Non-stop MARKETING; YOU ARE THE "ENERGIZER BUNNY".

29. Non-stop MARKETING; YOU ARE THE "ENERGIZER BUNNY".

30. Junior all-stars. A club for younger boys and girls with perhaps, special seating and a special game price. You get them on that mailing list and start them young. Cost is really nominal and set up the benefits including your logo'd t-shirt. You might be able to get a sponsor and perhaps have some "naming" rights to this group. A group like this has potential written all over them for your summer camps.

31. A sponsored bus trip to an away game. IF there's one game on the road where you can get tickets and your fans would like to go – work on scheduling such a trip.

32. Developing your press guide for each sport might be a "perk" for your season ticket holders. These are highly informative and have pictures and give all sorts of background information. Your season ticket holders should be the first to get these – and no charge.

... and this from the July 31, 2001, edition of USA TODAY:

"Louisville Brings Basketball Fans Closer to The Action. The University of Louisville has made 32 courtside seats for men's basketball at Freedom Hall available in what previously was a media area. The price: $15,000 a seat per season, with proceeds to go toward endowing athletic scholarships. Ten seats have been sold. Remaining are 20 sideline seats across from the team benches and 12 on the baseline next to the Cardinals bench. Several other schools have similar ticket plans. In April, Kentucky put 28 courtside seats on sale — two for a lifetime for $313,020."

The following excerpts were taken from the May 15, 2000, issue of SPORTS ILLUSTRATED an excellent article entitled: "Sit On It —The High Cost of Attending Games Is Fattening Owners' Wallets While It Drives Average Fans from Arenas, And It May Be Cooling America's Passion for Pro Sports", by E. M. Swift "Fan Reaction". SI commissioned the Peter Harris Research Group to conduct a scientific national survey of sports fans on issues related to attendance at major league baseball, NBA, NFL and NHL games. The 874 fans polled attended an average of 10.3 pro events OR college basketball or football games in the past year and 39.5 games in the past five years. Here are the top 10 reasons with percentages of fans citing them, that make respondents less likely to fill a seat at a sporting event today: The factors involved,

- Total cost to attend (57%
- Comfort of watching at home (41%)
- Players' behavior during games (41%) . Traffic and Parking (38%)
- Increase in sports on TV (35%). Lateness of games (26%)
- TV replay and analysis (22%)
- Unlikelihood of getting good seats (19%)
- Change in how local team is doing (14%)

- Change in family's interest in game (13%)

As we've mentioned, the sports fan has more and more choices; and in many cases, all of these choices conduct a heavy and costly marketing job on the consumer. In addition, at home, with the new 52" screen TV sets, you get more of an actual event – plus you've got that clicker in hand. If you don't have a good seat for the game, you stay at home.

With all the talk of the influence of TV on game attendance, we find that many of the sports TV ratings are down. So, we must really get to work to win fans back to our arenas/stadiums and address those objections.

What has become quite popular lately as a promotion, is RETRO NIGHT. It seems that it works better for basketball and baseball. I would imagine that a carryover to the students would bring additional interest. The cost with "retro" type uniforms would be prohibitive but everything else could revert back including prices at the concession stands, wearing apparel for the fans and any other ideas you might have. It would provide a "fun-type" atmosphere. It also might be worked around an alumni game and provide this as a double-header. This is a game in which you assess your schedule, if you feel that attendance will be "light", you could add this as a special incentive. There might be special type items that would fit into the "retro" theme that you could sell including t-shirts that might attract attention and blend in with the festivities.

CHAPTER 11

MOTIVATION AND ENCOURAGEMENT – YOUR SCOREBOARD

Throughout this book, we add to the "Filling Seats -Selling Seats" by stressing the importance of continuing to "BUILD FAN INTEREST". You continually look to find different ways to keep your team, coaches, and players in the LIMELIGHT — IN A POSITIVE MANNER. At the end of this chapter, we've included some information on our efforts at Northwestern University in getting local coaches and their players on campus to attend a basketball practice session. It's an excellent way to help you BUILD FAN INTEREST.

When it comes to motivation, it begins with SELF-MOTIVATION. If you have that quality, this will be a big help in your being a LEADER for your staff and others that will work WITH you. I've always liked the idea that my staff was OUR staff and they worked WITH me and not FOR me. I loved Marv Levy's quote on his coaching philosophy when he was inducted into the Pro Football Hall of Fame: "LEADERSHIP is the ability to get other people to get the best out of themselves. It's manifested by getting them not to follow you, but to JOIN you."

Your next phase of motivation is motivating your staff and your fans, So that's the big three in motivation. If you are a coach, you need to motivate your team as well as yourself, your staff, fans, and THE MEDIA. So, an important part of your job as the director of sports marketing is the motivation of your staff. I've always felt that leaders "lead" best by example. If you're a hard worker, come in early and stay late, you've got a head start. A "workaholic" is welcome but "WORKING SMART" shares in this equation.

I think your best results come from working to "BUILD A TEAM APPROACH" with your staff. Building becomes a large part in the development of teamwork – working together for a common goal and TRUSTING in each other. The more people you add to your staff, the more

> **If you are a coach, you need to motivate your team as well as yourself, your staff, fans, and THE MEDIA.**

you have to work at the "chemistry" of your group. Adding staff that will get along with each other and work together is a prerequisite for success.

I've always believed in "bulletin board" material. That would be those sayings and axioms that you believe in, and feel fit your situation for getting your philosophy across to your staff. I always liked a central bulletin board where your staff would see it. But on any written agendas for meetings, I would utilize an appropriate one at the top of the page or as a "thought for the day". I believe the written is more effective and fits better than verbalizing. It's amazing, that over the course of time, former staff will tell you that these were meaningful to their career and that they, personally use them. That's always a nice compliment and indicates that your time and effort to produce and repeat those were valuable to others.

A few axioms on teamwork might be:

"TEAM WORKS",

"There's no "I" in the word TEAM",

<u>T</u>ogether

<u>E</u>ach

<u>A</u>ccomplishes

<u>M</u>ore"

"TEAMWORK — Coming together is a BEGINNING

Keeping together is PROGRESS

Working together is SUCCESS"

"It's amazing how much can be accomplished if no one cares who gets the credit". From John Wooden's book regarding "Team Spirit" (p. 400), "No chain is stronger than its weakest link – no team is stronger than it's weakest player. One player attempting to grandstand can wreck the best team ever organized. We must be "one for all" and "all for one" with every player giving his very best every second of the game. The team is first, individual credit is second. There is no place for selfishness, egotism, or envy on our squad."

I've always liked to use the copy machine to give our players/staff "success" stories of championship teams/groups. This is good for <u>attitude development.</u> These are all effective motivators. However, don't use the theory of "one and done"; these can be repeated to be most effective and have a more lasting effect on your staff and their performance.

ENCOURAGEMENT is one of the more effective motivators that you can use.

ENCOURAGEMENT is one of the more effective motivators that you can use. In Ken Blanchard and Spencer Johnson's best seller, "The One Minute Manager", one portion had to do basically with "catching someone doing something right". I really felt his book had a great influence on many managers. This statement really hits home. This along with your teaching ability will be a successful approach to building your team. So make sure you not only encourage your marketing team but also compliment them – both pack a more powerful punch than anything else. Along with this, try to think of various ways whereby you can give your group and individuals within your group proper RECOGNITION. There are various methods of doing this. One might be a group picture that would be a part of the football or basketball press guide. Another might be the picture being placed in a football game program. It's a good feature story to put out to the media. When you speak at a luncheon or dinner, take one or two members of your team along with you and introduce. At any of the end-of-year banquets, make sure your staff is represented and acknowledged.

Now to your SCOREBOARD. We have mentioned this in a previous chapter, but want to go in to detail a little more at this time. This will serve as a terrific motivator for you and your staff. In addition, it has good public relations value because IF it's placed in a location for people to see, it helps build a good image/perception of what you and your group are trying to do. I don't feel that it should be in a real prominent location but someplace, probably in your office, where your staff will definitely see it and some others will also. You don't want to brag about the improvement in attendance nor do you want to showcase any downslide either.

You can put your Art Department to work to produce a nice looking bulletin board type display that you can easily put in numbers with your grease pen and easily wipe-off. The board should have a heading depicting your department and any "saying" or slogan you want at the top. What you need to do, if it's football, indicate a space for the placement of attendance figures for last year and a space next to it with this year's. You probably need to go back just the one year to the last season so the comparison can be made with this year. You'll probably want to go with total attendance. You must make the comparison based on the same standard for both years. You can indicate 1st, 2nd, 3rd, 4th, etc. and indicate the exact dates and opponent if you feel this is helpful. Many times, home openers draw better than others, so try to factor in all the variables that will make this effective and accurate. Of course, weather plays a part so if you want to have room for various factors like weather, opponent, league game, etc., try to do so. This board needs to probably be more practical than elaborate. It becomes a visible worksheet for your staff. They are going to try and "win" that attendance game and beat last year. Again, I think it is an excellent motivator and a gauge to see how effective you and your staff are performing. So give it a try. Again, your art department will be able to come up with an attractive looking "motivator" to assist the director of sports marketing. This board will be for home games and the more sports you are involved with, there will be a need for a scoreboard for each sport so the comparisons can be made.

When you are involved in filling seats as well as SELLING SEATS, you are also highly involved with BUILDING FAN INTEREST. I've mentioned before, I really liked the NBA's "one fan at a time" marketing campaign. At several schools, where I coached, I liked the idea of creating an inexpensive flyer that would be sent to all area high school and junior high school coaches. This flyer would invite the coaches to bring their players to a practice session, of course, free of charge. I always thought it was an excellent <u>public relations gesture.</u> The one thing I didn't do was get the names and addresses of all of the attendees. Of course, we knew the coaches and their schools but somehow we needed to get those names and addresses (also e-mail) of their players in attendance. Why? They would be great candidates to receive information in the future on schedules, ticket information and also basketball camp brochures. If they attend the practice, they have now been on campus and at least seen a little portion of our campus and the facilities, and of course, know of our location. This FLYER sent out to the area coaches had other benefits — it had pictures of the entire coaching staff and of course, the "invitation" to come to practice and bring players. It didn't end with this. We had our managers, in all our practice sessions, armed with copies of our practice schedule for that particular day, a pocket schedule, how to join our "Fast Break Club" and summer camp information for the upcoming year. This was all in a small packet form with school colors, follow the Wildcats, Chicago's Big Ten team, and the full nine yards. If we could spare one of the assistant coaches, they could go up in to the stands and meet and greet. They could also explain some of the drills that we were using. ALSO, in the packet of information was a page with the roster of the players at that practice and their number, year in school, home town, high school, etc. The following two pages have a copy of this flyer – use colored paper – and SELL.

(Front Panel)

THE NORTHWESTERN WILDCAT BASKETBALL STAFF......

HEAD COACH BILL FOSTER

BILL DONLON

QUITMAN SULLINS

TIM CARTER

SHAWN PARRISH

INVITE you....

NORTHWESTERN UNIVERSITY BASKETBALL SCHEDULE 1991-1992

SAT., OCT. 26	Abbreviated PURPLE/WHITE GAME 11-11:50am (just prior to our ILLINOIS home football game in WELSH-RYAN ARENA)		
WED., NOV. 13	MARATHON OIL (Exhibition Game)	7:00p	CST
MON., NOV. 18	BRAZIL (Exhibition Game)	8:00p	CST
FRI., NOV. 22	ILLINOIS WESLEYAN	7:00p	CST
SAT., NOV. 30	COLUMBIA UNIVERSITY	7:30p	CST
MON., DEC. 2	VANDERBILT UNIVERSITY	7:00p	CST
WED., DEC. 4	Tulane University	7:00p	CST
SAT., DEC. 14	NORTHEASTERN UNIVERSITY	7:00p	CST
MON., DEC. 16	IDAHO STATE	7:00p	CST
SAT., DEC. 21	Loyola University (Rosemont Horizon)	1:00p	CST
FRI., DEC. 27	Arizona State Tournament		
	NU vs. Creighton	6:00p	CST
	ASU vs. Brown		
SAT., DEC. 28	Arizona State/Tribune Classic Championship Game	6/8:00p	CST
MON., JAN. 6	UNIVERSITY OF CHICAGO	7:00p	CST
WED., JAN. 8	@ Wisconsin	7:00p	CST
SAT., JAN. 11	OHIO STATE	7:00p	CST
WED., JAN. 15	@ Michigan State	8:00p	EST
SAT., JAN. 18	INDIANA	7:00p	CST
WED., JAN. 22	IOWA	7:00p	CST
SAT., JAN. 25	@ Purdue	8:00p	EST
WED., JAN. 29	@ Minnesota	7:00p	CST
SAT., FEB. 1	ILLINOIS	7:00p	CST
WED., FEB. 5	@ Michigan	8:00p	EST
SAT., FEB. 8	MINNESOTA	7:00p	CST
SAT., FEB. 15	@ Indiana	3:00p	EST
THU., FEB. 20	PURDUE	7:00p	CST
SAT., FEB. 22	MICHIGAN	Noon	CST
WED., FEB. 26	@ Illinois	7:00pm	CST
THU., MAR. 5	MICHIGAN STATE (ESPN)	6:30p	CST
SAT., MAR. 7	@ Ohio State	3:00p	EST
WED., MAR. 11	@ Iowa	7:00p	EST
SAT., MAR. 14	WISCONSIN	7:00p	CST

To Our Beautiful Evanston Campus!

NORTHWESTERN UNIVERSITY

MCGAW HALL
1501 CENTRAL STREET
EVANSTON, IL 60208
708-491-7904

Practice Schedule
NU Basketball
1991-92 Season

OCTOBER:

Tuesday	October 15	3:30-6:00pm
Wednesday	October 16	3:30-6:00pm
Thursday	October 17	3:30-6:00pm
Friday	October 18	3:30-6:00pm
Saturday	October 19	9:30-12:00noon
Sunday	*October 20*	*NO PRACTICE*
Monday	October 21	3:30-6:00pm
Tuesday	October 22	3:30-6:00pm
Wednesday	October 23	3:30-6:00pm
Thursday	*October 24*	*NO PRACTICE*
Friday	October 25	3:30-6:00pm
Saturday	October 26	9:45-12:00noon

PURPLE & WHITE GAME
11-11:50 AM (FREE)

Sunday	October 27	7:00-9:30pm
Monday	October 28	3:30-6:00pm
Tuesday	*October 29*	*NO PRACTICE*
Wednesday	October 30	3:30-6:00pm
Thursday	October 31	3:30-6:00pm

NOVEMBER:

Friday	November 1	3:30-6:00pm
Saturday	November 2	9:30-12:00noon
Sunday	November 3	7:00-9:30pm
Monday	*November 4*	*NO PRACTICE*
Tuesday	November 5	3:30-6:00pm
Wednesday	November 6	3:30-6:00pm
Thursday	November 7	6:30-9:00pm **DICK VITALE NIGHT**
Friday	November 8	3:30-6:00pm
Saturday	November 9	9:30-12:00noon
Sunday	*November 10*	*NO PRACTICE*
Monday	November 11	3:30-6:00pm
Tuesday	November 12	3:30-6:00pm
Wednesday	November 13	**MARATHON OIL**
Thursday	November 14	3:30-6:00pm
Friday	*November 15*	*NO PRACTICE*
Saturday	November 16	9:30-12:00noon
Sunday	November 17	7:00-9:30pm
Monday	November 18	**BRAZIL**
Tuesday	November 19	3:30-6:00pm
Wednesday	November 20	3:30-6:00pm
Thursday	November 21	3:30-6:00pm
Friday	November 22	**ILL. WESLEYAN**

(on reverse side)

Dear Coach:

Here's our practice schedule up to our home exhibition games - November 13th (MARATHON OIL) and November 18th (BRAZIL NATIONAL TEAM).

Our practice sessions are always open and we would be pleased to have you, your staff and players be our guests at any time. Please call Shawn Parrish in our office in advance so we know when to expect you.

Also, complimentary tickets are available to players and coaches on a limited basis for our home contests in November and December. Tickets to our conference games are also available, but since many are sold out we are more restricted. Please call well in advance to inquire about availability.

CHICAGO'S BIG TEN TEAM

This flyer was folded so we had three panels and we used regular 8½ by 11" paper — we used light purple stock (purple being Northwestern's school color). This was folded to fit into a regular number ten envelope. If you want to involve more information going out to the coaches, you can use the legal size 8½ by 14" paper and have one more fold in it to fit into a number ten envelope. As in all other mail-outs, fill up that one ounce that the post office gives you for first class mail. If you are a high school, you can adapt the same idea to bringing in your elementary school and/or junior high school teams in a similar arrangement. You can have your players meet and greet after practice as well as the entire coaching staff. It's always good to follow up with a letter to that coach saying "thanks" for coming to practice and sending any other information on your program that will fit into that one ounce that the postal department gives us.

Together

Each

Accomplishes

More

PATIENCE — "Good things cometh to he who waiteth <u>IF</u> he worketh like heck while he waiteth"

"It's a <u>WE</u> team . . . Not a <u>ME</u> team"

While we're wrapping up this chapter, I wanted to get to just a few of the DESIRED ATTRIBUTES of the sports marketing director. When I think of this I think of several things. First, I believe it was Emerson's quote that I loved: "Nothing Great Was Ever Achieved Without ENTHUSIASM". I was really lucky at Northwestern University to have one of the best, if not the best in marketing – Don MacLachlan, who has since gone on to become the Sr. Vice President of the Tennessee Titans in the NFL. Don had great enthusiasm and optimism combined with being highly intelligent with a super personality and work ethic. I was so lucky to have been able to work with him. Emerson must have been thinking about Don when he made that statement. In addition, Don's "energy tank" was always at FULL.

NOTES

CHAPTER 12

IDEAS FROM OTHERS

In this chapter – we are indebted to the people who answered our survey... that can show others what is going on in various sports with their marketing. We THANK each of them for their time, and ideas that they shared with all of us. Here's the five questions we asked to use as GUIDELINES for our survey:

1) Your most effective marketing promotion for season ticket sales? List your top two.

2) Your two most successful single game promotions (in terms of ticket sale response?)

3) Your two most successful marketing tools to get more students to attend games?

4) One thought to better promote your 2000-2001 season that you didn't do last season?

5) Any final comments regarding your sports marketing?

Again, my SINCERE THANKS to each of the individuals and teams/schools that shared their thoughts and ideas with us. So, here we go in alphabetical order:

CHARLESTON RIVERDOGS

PO BOX 20849 • CHARLESTON • SC 29413 • 843.723.7241 • FAX 843.723.2641

To: Bill Foster

From: Mike Veeck, President

Re: Filling Seats = Dollars

Date: October 30, 2000

1. Your most effective marketing promotion for season ticket sales? LIST TOP TWO.
   Our most effective marketing promotion for season tickets are:
   a. Radio commercial in which we mentioned each new subscriber By Name in humorous fashion. Charlestonians love recognition.
   b. The bar code mailer. See attached.

2. Your two most successful single game promotions (in terms of ticket sale response):
   a. Tonya Harding Mini Bat Night - Ms. Harding made a personal appearance.
   b. A media Frenzy.

3. Your two most successful marketing tools to get more students to attend games?
   a. Thirsty Thursdays with theme cheaper beer.
   b. Handbills on campus with rep.

4. One thought to better promote your 2000-2001 season that you didn't do last season (colleges – pick a sport).
   More attention given to the season ticket campaign. Business to business and consumer direct mail pieces. Historically, a weak area in our marketing plan.

5. Any final comments regarding your sports marketing?
   The Internet is going to change everything. We sell etix.com. We broadcast on the net. We are going to billboards (or back, if you will). Technology actually is, I believe, going to help the baseball business. Faster commerce means a yearning for a simpler, slower time. We could be on the cusp if we don't blow it.

AFFILIATE OF THE TAMPA BAY DEVIL RAYS

ATTENTION: This postcard may be redeemed for $1 off ticket price for one of the final 7 home games.*

Celebrate Seven Lucky Days at the Birdcage!

Seven Lucky Days...Hundreds of Possible Winners!

Bring this postcard to the Birdcage and we'll scan the bar code to see if you're an instant winner! We're celebrating our last seven home games at Sioux Falls Stadium before the newly renovated stadium opens in May of 2000.

Win a Chance to Watch A Canaries Game From a Birds-Eye View!

Our Grand Prize Winner and Guests Get A **FREE** Night in a Luxury Suite at the Newly Renovated Stadium in the Summer of 2000!

Up to 500 instant winners may receive an official Canaries sweatshirt ($30 value). All redeemed winning postcards will be entered in the Grand Prize drawing to be held during Fan Appreciation Night on September 1st.

(Need not be present to win Grand Prize. Odds of being one of 500 instant winners: 1 in 100.)

Simply bring your card to the front gate of the stadium during our last seven home games (8/18, 8/19, 8/20, 8/21, 8/22, 8/31 and 9/1) to determine if you are a winner. Cards will be scanned one hour prior to game time until 2 hours after start of game. All games start at 7:05 PM except Sundays game which starts at 6:05. There is no ticket purchase necessary to win.

* Limit 4 tickets. Based on availability.

186

0 780648455779 6 007

CHICAGO CUBS
WRIGLEY FIELD
1060 W. Addison Street
Chicago, Illinois 60613-4397

From Frank Maloney
Director of Ticket Operations

1. Most effective marketing promotion for season ticket sales?

    a. Full-page ad with schedule in major newspaper is most effective for season ticket sales.

    b. We have a high season-ticket base with little inventory to sell, therefore, we do not discount or do any special promotion with marginal inventory.

2. Two most successful single-game promotions?

    a. Beanie Baby (TyCo) promotions to children under 12 by far our best most recent promotion.

    b. 70's night featuring 70's music and encourage wearing of 70's garb.

3. Two most successful marketing tools to get more students to attend games?

    a. School promotion -- heavily discount tickets on selected dates where seats projected to go unsold.

    b. Have championship teams from schools singing our 7th inning, "Take Me Out To The Ball Game"

4. Thoughts to Better Promote for the 2000-2001 Season?

    a. A better team/record makes our job much easier.

5. Any further comments on Sports Marketing?

    We sell Wrigley Field and the "experience" - we sell the neighborhood; "spend the day in Wrigleyville" - rather than just the game; we sell the nostalgia, the Ivy, and the pristine atmosphere.

(Ed. note: You have to go to a game in Wrigley Field -- it IS a unique experience and a terrific atmosphere)

EL PASO DIABLOS

A Brand New Ball Game

Effective means of Promoting Season Ticket Sales

The El Paso Diablos implemented a new and unique season ticket package during the 2000 season, "Making Dreams Come True." To become a member of the "Making Dreams Come True" group, a company was required to purchase a minimum of 10 full season tickets. The company could then use the tickets at its' discretion for a variety of purposes, such as entertaining clients, employee rewards or just to have for baseball enthusiasts. Any tickets that the company did not use were given to a Diablos representative who distributed them to the different non-profit children's groups that exist in El Paso and the surrounding area. Each night a company donated tickets, a special announcement was made thanking the organization for its' support of the El Paso community.

El Paso Diablos' season ticket holders receive many benefits that are not provided in any other packages. Season ticket holders are the core support group of the franchise and should be treated in a special way. The season ticket holders receive Arizona Diamondbacks spring training tickets, food and concession coupons, guaranteed giveaways, and the right of first refusal on their seats for special events, along with many other exciting promotions that occur throughout the season.

Single Game Promotions

When marketing major events and entertainment for the upcoming season, the Diablos take into account tradition and the latest fads of the time. For example, fireworks shows and the Famous Chicken are widely viewed as the premiere events to attend. Both promotions take place multiple times throughout the season and many fans plan their trips to the ball park based on these two promotions. We have found that having six fireworks shows and the Famous Chicken on three occasions allows the fans of El Paso a great opportunity to enjoy each of these fantastic events more than once. The biggest concern is to make sure the dates are properly positioned and properly spaced out.

It is always necessary to promote an event based upon the fad of the times. As an example, this past season our organization built one of the world's largest pinatas. Pinatas are extremely popular in El Paso with people of all ages. The key to the events' success however, was that the pinata was constructed as the Pokemon character Pikachu. Pokeman cards and characters were one of the hottest sellers with kids of all ages over the past two summers and this promotion encouraged children of all ages to come and see something out of the ordinary. The pinata promotion is a perfect example of a way to attract people who normally don't come to the ballpark. The El Paso Diablos have also had tremendous success in drawing people to Cohen Stadium with special promotions, including appearances by the Rugrats, Sesame Street characters, midget wrestlers along with giveaways, including Pokeman cards, hats, bats and baseball cards.

Promoting your Team

The key to successfully promoting your team to potential attendees is choosing promotions that will allow the staff to have fun and get excited. The team needs to maintain an exciting and upbeat atmosphere that the staff can be proud of. The positive atmosphere will carry itself from your offices to the people that are sitting in the seats and should begin as soon as they walk through the gates. People want to feel excited about what is happening when they enter the park and it is incumbent upon team employees to create an atmosphere that shows your venue is the place to be. Fans attend games because they want to relax, spend time with friends and family and enjoy themselves. It is our job as sports administrators to make sure fans are put in an atmosphere that is clean, safe, and exciting! Treat your fans as if they are family and never forget that without their support, your team doesn't exist.

Burke McKinney, M.A.
Assistant General Manager

9700 Gateway North Blvd. • P.O. Drawer 4797 • El Paso, Texas 79914
(915) 755-2000 Phone • (915) 757-0671 Fax
www.diablos.com
AA Affiliate of the Arizona Diamondbacks

QUAD CITY MALLARDS

P.O. BOX 1003 / 1509 3RD AVENUE A / MOLINE, ILLINOIS 61265
309-764-PUCK (7825) / FAX 309-764-7858
www.qcmallards.com

1997 Colonial Cup Champions • 1998 Tarry Cup Champions • 1998 Colonial Cup Champions • Member United Hockey League

Howard Cornfield
Vice President Hockey Operations
United Sports Ventures
Phone (309) 764-7825   Fax (309) 737-2519
E-Mail: Headduck@qcmallards.com

1. Our Most Effective Marketing Promotion for Season Ticket Sales.
   a. From the start of our franchise, we included free playoff tickets with the purchase of season tickets. Although I initially disliked the program, I am now a believer. It was the impetus behind raising our full season ticket packages to over 3,600. As time has gone on, we have tightened certain requirements:
      1. 50% deposits are due no later than February 1 of each year.
      2. Tickets must be paid in full by March 31 of each year.
   People who don't meet these requirements lose the free playoff ticket privilege.

   We enjoy having money in hand for next season before we even complete the current season. Our season tickets are not discounted so this is the special bonus seasonticketholders receive. There will be times (like over the past four seasons) when we play up to 11 playoff games and that is a tremendous value for our fans.

   We now have a very limited period for people to sign up for new season tickets and still receive free playoff tickets; otherwise, the offer has been closed and seen as a reward for our loyal fans.

   b. We have started a fan loyalty card that will reward season ticketholders with valuable prizes for attending our games and supporting our sponsors. Developed with the thought of providing our fans with another value added incentive, the "Quacker Backer" card will also help us to better define our demographics, tell us where they shop, eat, vacation and even their favorite local newspapers and casino and so on. This will in turn aid our corporate sponsorship efforts because we will be able to show hard facts to our potential sponsors and we will encourage our sponsors to reward our fans with special deals and discounts.

2. Most Successful Single Game Promotions.
   a. A family night promotion that we call "Critter Night" is a fan favorite. It features local and national mascots that spend the evening roaming the stands culminating with a between periods broomball game between the "Animal Critters" and the "Food Critters". Involving approximately 30 mascots, this is a cheap promotion that provides lots of enjoyment for families. This is also another way to motivate corporate sponsors to participate with the team because we do not allow local mascots who do not participate as a corporate sponsor to participate in the promotion.

   b. The annual "Church Night" promotions that Bill Foster introduced me to are another strong promo. We bring in a major celebrity to speak with the group before the game and then the celebrity signs autographs after the talk.

   c. Other strong promos for us have included bringing in comic book heros such as the Power Rangers or Batman and also we have had success with bringing in race car drivers.

3. Successful Marketing Tools To Get Students To Games.
   a. Students like free things....our most successful promos for them include providing a free buffet usually consisting of donated hot dogs, popcorn, soft drinks and even $1.00 beers.
   b. Another strong promotion was "Valentines Day for the Broken Hearted" in which we paired up lonely students with other lonely students with the help of local DJs and contests we did at the game.

4. Better Promote Our Upcoming Season.
   a. We are purchasing several of the extra large, visible billboards in town with the changeable letters that will allow us to daily update the board with upcoming promotions, games and even scores. We will have sponsors who will also participate with the boards by having their logos on them.

5. Final Thoughts.
We are entering our sixth year as one of the premier minor league hockey organizations in the country and it has become apparent that we must continue to re-invent ourselves or the fans will get bored. Our promotions must be newer, our game presentation must be refreshed and even though our players have always been accessible, they must be MORE accessible.

Our fans have become spoiled; they expect to win every game and they expect to win championships each year. This makes it imperative that our efforts off the ice be superlative because the time will come that through injuries or misfortune, we may struggle. Without a first rate marketing / promotional operation already in progress that doesn't depend solely on winning, a situation like this could be disastrous for a professional franchise.

Department of Athletics

University of Louisville
Louisville, Kentucky 40292
(502) 852-5732
FAX: (502) 852-0816

UNIVERSITY of LOUISVILLE

Brian Levey
University of Louisville
Assistant Athletic Director - Marketing and Promotions
Phone (502) 852-0860
Fax (502) 852-0816

FOOTBALL

1) The most effective marketing promotion for season ticket sales.
    a) Family Plan. In this section of the Papa John's Cardinal Stadium endzone, regular ticket price is $175 per ticket without any type of donation. Using the Family Plan special, a family of four can purchase season tickets for $455 (regular price $700).
    b) Opponents. Although the marketing department does not control scheduling, popular opponents bring fans!

2) Successful single game promotions.
    a) Top 10 for $10. The week of each home game we release any unsold endzone tickets in the top 10 rows of Papa John's Cardinal Stadium for $10 each, a savings of $15 off the regular price of $25.

3) Successful marketing tools for students.
    a) Discounted season tickets, almost half price, to those returning students that purchase their tickets prior to May 1. This special is also offered to incoming freshman based on availability through their orientation.
    b) We offer the student the ability to purchase a guest ticket for a discounted rate on both a season and individual game basis. This not only allows the student to purchase tickets for friends and family members but gives them the ability to sit with their guest in the student area of Papa John's Cardinal Stadium.

4) One thought to better promote U of L Football in the future.
    a) We need to utilize the assets of our media partners better. Not only use the TV or radio spots we have but take advantage of things like community event calendars, interviews with coaches and players, call-in shows, etc.

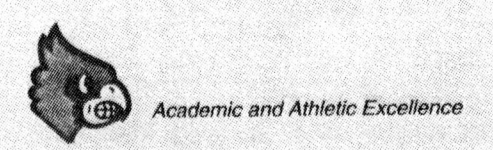

Academic and Athletic Excellence

LYCOMING COLLEGE
WILLIAMSPORT, PENNSYLVANIA 17701

Department of Athletics

(570) 321-4020
1-800-333-5926

September 6, 2000

Bill Foster
PO Box 2329
Coppell, TX 75019-8329

Dear Coach Foster,

In response to your survey:

1.) We don't do season ticket sales at Division III. I don't know of any Division III school that does.

2.) A. **Alumni Day**
Any alum attending is admitted FREE. They just pay for their spouse (if not an alum) and their children. This is always one of our best days at the concession stand.
B. **"Future Warriors Day"**
Any student under the age of 18 – wearing their high school, junior high school, Pop Warner, etc. football game jersey is admitted FREE. This is our largest concession stand day at 25-30% of them will now bring a paying adult.

3.)

4.) Basketball – Do a 50-50 raffle. The winner can win the entire amount by making 2 out of 3 free throws at ½ time.

Robb Curry
Associate Athletic Director

LYCOMING WARRIORS

NCAA DIVISION III   M.A.C.

MILWAUKEE BREWERS BASEBALL CLUB

from: Bob Voight
Vice President - Ticket Sales
E-Mail: BOBV@milwaukeebrewers.com

1. Your most effective marketing promotion for season ticket sales?

    a. guaranteed and priority seat location in Miller Park (2001)
    b. Season ticket discounts

2. Your two most successful single-game promotions?

    a. Spring Madness
    b. Bank One Family Days

3. Most successful marketing tools to get more students to attend games?

    a. Advertising campaign: integrated campaign featuring "can't beat the fun at the old ballpark" and "final year in Milwaukee County Stadium"
    b. Marketing to women and families. Affordable Family Fun.

4. One thought to better promote your 2000-2001 season that you didn't do last season?

    a. Emphasize Miller Park: "Old fashioned feel" of traditional ballpark coupled with modern customer amenities and convenience.

5. Any final comments regarding your sports marketing?

    1. We are in the entertainment business not the sports business. Any leisure-time activity is our competition.

(Ed. Note: Bob Voight sent along several of their printed brochures/packets which were very impressive -- the one on the "Party Suites" makes you want to call up immediately and purchase or rent a suite -- it looks so inviting and a super way to entertain guests/friends.)

From: Gary Saunders, Asst. General Manager, Myrtle Beach Pelicans, Carolina League Class "A" Affiliate of the Atlanta Braves, Year 2000. 1251 - 21st Avenue N, Myrtle Beach, SC 29577. (843) 918-6014

1. Most Effective Marketing Promotion for Season Ticket Sales: "For us, nothing beats that personal contact: Door to Door; Networking and referrals; keep it simple; elbow grease.

2. Two most successful single game promotions (in terms of ticket sales):

    People here at the beach love giveaway nights, especially baseballs (Limited edition), youth dates, etc. Appearances by the famous Chicken, the Blues Brothers, etc. -- must be heavily promoted and sponsored to insure success.

3. Two most successful marketing tools to get more students to attend games?

    1. Career Day -- weekday game; educational
    2. Fund Raisers - schools sell ticket at face value, keep $2.50 for their cause.

4. Thoughts to Better promote your 2000-2001 season that you didn't do last season?

    Adopt more flexible ticket packages. Allow fans to choose games (5-10-20-25 game ticket plans) that best fit their schedules

5. Any final comments regarding your sports marketing?

    Award or reward fans who attend with high frequency. We have a "frequent Flyer" plan which rewards season ticket holders who attend often. Incentives include jackets, polo shirts, hats, and other logo'd items.

Myrtle Beach Pelicans
Carolina League Class "A" Affiliate of the Atlanta Braves

Gary Saunders
Assistant General Manager

1251 21st Ave. N. • Myrtle Beach, SC 29577
843.918.6014 • Fax 843.918.6001
www.myrtlebeachpelicans.com • gsaunders@mb-baseball.com

On the back of Gary's business card was the following:

   For Ticket Information:
   (843) 918-6000

   For Group Sales:
   (843) 918-6020

(Ed. Note: I personally met with Gary at their ballpark; he was most helpful and friendly. I loved their "2000 Group Outings & Picnic Packages, Pelicans Fun For Your Flock" poster -- in addition to being most attractive and eye catching, it had so much information printed on it.

Department of Athletics Archbishop Moeller High School
9001 Montgomery Road, Cincinnati, Ohio 45242   (513) 792-3340   Fax (513) 792-3356

Dick Beerman - Co-Athletic Directors
Barry Borman - Co-Athletic Directors

1. Your most effective marketing promotion for season ticket sales - LIST TOP TWO.

   We send out a season ticket mailing to approximately 1500 addresses currently - football only: This constitutes all families currently enrolled in Grades 9-12, the families with sons entering the 9th grade in the fall, plus all Booster Club members.

   We plan to add a mailing next year to all <u>graduates</u> who played football.

2. Your two most successful single game promotions (in terms of ticket sale response):

   It has become a very regular fact that at least two of our games each season have become sellout (i.e. 9,000-12,000) size crowds. No promotion is necessary!

3. Your two most successful marketing tools to get more students to attend games?

   For our own school and quite commonly for the other three (all male) schools which constitute the Catholic League (South) in Cincinnati, the pride, tradition and almost unbelievable level of State and National Success motivates our communities to consistently support us in an outstanding manner.

4. One thought to better promote your 2000-2001 season that you didn't do last seasons (college - pick a sport).

   We are currently working to develop a "Press Guide" type profile for all thirteen (13) of our Varsity sports covering all of the years, athletes, records, statistics (when available) and in some cases an indication of the College and Professional success of our graduates. E.g. eight have played major League Baseball, including two MVPs Barry Larken & Ken Griffey Jr.

5. Any final comments regarding your sports marketing?

   As a high school entity, we can only try to cooperate with any and all media and interested parties who are willing to assist us to present Archbishop Moeller in a positive way. We do our best to respect the need for timely and accurate response to all requests. We have no budget to promote ourselves. We are blessed with high quality, first-class coaches, parents and athletes who serve to market our school and our Athletic Program.

Prepared by: Bill McGillis (Sr. Associate Athletic Director) and the Marketing Staff, University of New Mexico, Albuquerque, NM 87131-0001

LOBO MEN'S BASKETBALL MARKETING PLAN
(LAST UPDATED, SEPTEMBER 18, 2000)

GOALS
A. Sell Record Number of Season Tickets
   14,262 record (1999)
B. Average Attendance: 17,300 (Top 10 nationally)
   17,507 record (1997-98)
   17,065 (1999-2000) (16,443 with Postseason NIT) (8th nationally)
C. Revenue: $4 million ($4.5 million with concessions / novelties)
   $3,757,529 last year ($4,281,574 with concessions / novelties)
D. Continually Improve Game Atmosphere
E. Sellout Game Sponsorships, Signage and On Court Promotional Opportunities

I. SEASON TICKET SALES

A. Renewals – The best way to maintain our high season ticket number is to retain our current season ticket holders. The goal will be retain 95% of the 1999-2000 season ticket holders. After the initial renewal, two follow-up reminder postcards will be sent by the ticket office. Additionally, selected Lobo Club Fund Drive workers will lead a phone-a-thon to renew the remainder of unrenewed season ticket holders.

B. Student Season Ticket Policy Change – The attached memo will allow for an increase in season ticket holders. In past years, students not only had the opportunity to purchase season tickets for themselves, but also were permitted to purchase one additional season ticket at regular price. This year, students may purchase one additional season ticket at a discounted rate plus two more at regular price. Giving students this opportunity should increase season ticket numbers plus revenue. This will be promoted through direct email to UNM students, flyers to UNM student groups, greeks, residential life and numerous ads in the Daily Lobo.

C. Media Push – A detailed media plan (attached) will emphasize that season tickets are available. The "myth" that The Pit is sold out at every game needs to be set straight and television, radio and print advertising will dispel that false rumor.

D. On-Air Interviews – We will utilize three or four of our allotted 36 Citadel On-Air Interviews to discuss the fact that season tickets are available and the means to obtain those tickets.

E. Telesports – The UNM Athletics Department hired Telesports (a New York based sports telemarketing company) to assist with selling tickets. It is believed that our department should generate a large majority of the new season ticket sales, however Telesports can come in at the last minute to sell any tickets that are a difficult sales (i.e. top 3 rows in the benches behind the basket and scattered singles)

F. Direct Sales Calls to Current Season Ticket Holders – Last year more than 200 season tickets were unsold because they were scattered singles. If time permits, calls can be made to people sitting next to those unsold tickets to encourage them to purchase that additional ticket.

G. Faculty / Staff Mailer – A direct mail flyer will be sent to all UNM Faculty and Staff letting them know of the 50% discount they receive as UNM employees.

H. Select-A-Seat – In conjunction with the annual Lobo Howl. The best (or remaining) season tickets will be marked for a "first come, first serve" sale.

II. AVERAGE ATTENDANCE

A. Student Season Ticket Policy Change – The attached memo will allow for an increase in overall ticket sales. In past years, students were permitted to purchase single game tickets until 10 days prior to the game. On most games, this meant 10 days prior to the game, seats were available when previously there were only Standing Room Only Tickets. Now single game tickets will be available for purchase in the beginning of the season and the hopes of having a complete sellout for games in advance will increase.

B. Media Game Sponsorships – Due to the fact that only one game completely sold out in 1999-2000, we have added radio and television partners on many games, especially those that have the opportunity to sellout, but may need a "little push", especially to sell all Standing Room Tickets. Each media partner will run $12,000 in airtime plus have ticket giveaways to create excitement and a buzz surrounding the event.

C. Youth Day – The Marketing Department will implement a Youth Day event during the Comcast Lobo Invitational in late December. Youths (18 and under) will receive admission for $5 (Standing Room Only). This will be heavily promoted and encourage attendance during the Holiday Season when attendance is normally light.

III. GAME ATMOSPHERE

The Marketing Department will, as always, constantly try to improve fan entertainment at Lobo events, including new music from the computer and band. With the addition of a new music computer and band director, we look at add many new songs to Lobo Basketball Gameday. Plus, the spirit squad numbers and talent are improving to further add to a positive outing at UNM Basketball games. Furthermore, halftime entertainment will be a point of emphasis. Some local acts will be asked to provided a routine at halftime, while some national performances will be scheduled to perform.

III. **PROMOTIONS**

The following is a list of season long promotions planned for the 2000-2001 season:
- A. Western Union Starting Lineup
- B. Wendy's Soundmeter – Prizes provided for fans if the highest level is obtained 75 times
- C. Southwest Airlines Hot and Cold Contest – on court halftime contest
- D. Pizza Hut "Fan of the Game" Promotion
- E. Pepsi / Las Vegas – Lobo Rollers Timeout Promotion
- F. Pizza Hut Blimp
- G. Pennzoil at the Half Promotion
- H. Outback Steakhouse - On Court Timeout Promotion
- I. McDonalds Ball Kids of the Game Promotion
- J. Garduno's Sombrero Toss - Timeout Promotion
- K. Earthgrains Little Lobo of the Game
- L. Comcast Slingshots - Timeout Promotion
- M. Bank of America - On court Timeout Promotion
- N. Bank of America Coaches Tips of the game
- O. Baillio's Beat the Clock Contest - Timeout On Court Promotion
- P. Alltel Three Point Shot Contest - Timeout On Court Promotion
- Q. Lanier Halftime Statistics
- R. Intel Scores For Scholars
- S. Furrs Favorite Player
- T. American Airlines Player of the Game Promotion
- U. DKD Electric Lights Out Shooter of the Game
- V. Albuquerque Journal College Scoreboard Update

IV. **ADVERTISING**

The Marketing Department will implement the following advertising:
- 300,000 Schedule Cards
- 5,000 Schedule Posters
- 2,000 Autograph Cards
- 8,000 Team Trading Cards
- Marquee Board Announcements
- Television: $36,000 (season tickets campaign)
  - Comcast - $15,000
  - KOB TV Channel 4 - $6,000
  - KRQE News 13 - $15,000
- Radio: $50,000 (season tickets campaign)
  - 610 The Sports Animal - $5,000
  - AGM - $10,000
  - Arrow 102.5 - $10,000
  - ClearChannel Communications - $10,000
  - NewsRadio 770 KKOB - $10,000
  - 101.3 The Bone - $5,000

Print:
- Albuquerque Journal – 75 column inches (60 with women)
- Daily Lobo – 4 half page ads
- New Mexico Business Weekly – 6 half page ads
- Donrey Outdoor – 3 months usage of 4 color highway billboard
- Bowlin – 6 weeks of 2 color pony panels (30 boards)

Promotional Plans and Strategies

1. The most successful single game promotion (ticket sales)

We will be pitching the following idea to businesses in the Pittsburgh area.

Companies can have their own "Tailgate" event prior to and during a Robert Morris home game. The Human Resources department will be our first contact. Essentially, we will provide food, beverages and a section of seats for the company in exchange for a ticket package – price to be determined. Part of the money generated will go to charity and the rest will go to our department. It is a great opportunity for a company to allow their employees to interact in a less stressful environment and to watch some great basketball.

2. Two most successful marketing tools to get more students to attend games.

Residence Challenge

Our residence is broken up into sections. With this promotion we will create a competitive environment between the different sections. Who cheers the loudest – Who dresses up the craziest – Who has the best cheer. No matter what the contest, we want to create some energy at the game and make students believe they can have a great time at our games. The section that wins the contest gets a pizza party!

Tuition Give-away

With the rising cost of tuition, every student is looking for ways to earn scholarships and decrease their expenses. Students can get one-semester of tuition covered by attending the game and winning a competition. It may be as simple as a draw or several students could be selected to shoot from half court for the prize. Regardless, students will get charged up about this event!

3. Better promotion for the 2000-2001 season

This season we are initiating a Guest Coach program. Alumni, Faculty Members and other key stakeholders of the program will be offered the chance to take part in our game day events as a guest coach. They will attend our pre-game meal, meetings and sit on the bench (behind, beside) during the game. We have also used this program as a fund raising strategy at our yearly auction.

4. Final comments regarding marketing

As a staff, we believe that there is nothing limiting our program. If we want to put the work into a plan, then we can do it and it will be successful. However, if some of the initiatives that are listed above are not done professionally then the public will choose to take their time and their entertainment dollar elsewhere. We need to create opportunities for the public that are convenient and fun!

Ron Wuotila
Coordinator of Basketball Operations

Ed. Note: Ron Wuotila recently moved on to become Director of Operations for Women's Basketball, University of Pittsburgh, Fitzgerald Field House, Pittsburgh, PA 15261 (1-800-404-HOOP

RUSS POTTS PRODUCTIONS, INC.

November 1, 2000

Bill Foster, President
BF Sports
P.O. Box 2329
Coppell, TX 75019-8329

Dear Bill:

In response to your questionnaire:

1) The most effective marketing promotion for season ticket sales:

   (a) *Mustang Mania* campaign built around a total media, radio and TV station trade, and corporate partners program at SMU

   (b) *Winning Spree in '73* campaign at the University of Maryland building upon the tradition of Maryland football and new coach Jerry Claiborne - also a media blitz type campaign

2) The two most successful single game promotions:

   (a) *Baptist and Methodist Youth Day* - Baylor - SMU game - largest crowd in the history of the eighty year series between Baylor and SMU, over 65,000 at the stadium. We developed phone banks and a mail campaign for all Baptist and Methodist youth, in Texas, Oklahoma and Louisiana.

   (b) *McDonald's Kids Day* - Maryland vs. Villanova - five kids free with each paying adult. Had a huge concession day, largest in Maryland football history -1973.

3) The two most successful marketing tools to get more students to attend games:

   (a) Strong media blitz
   (b) Television, radio and newspaper campaigns

14 North Braddock Street • Winchester, VA 22601 • 540-665-0598
FAX # 540-665-8399

(4)   One thought to better promote the 2000-01 season that wasn't done last season (colleges -pick a sport)

Not applicable

(5)   Final comments:

I was the first Sports Marketing Director in college athletics. Now there are over 300. Created the first commercial scoreboard sales at Maryland, created the Terrapin Radio Network, the largest printed program in the nation - 240 pages, created the two campaigns at Maryland and SMU that resulted in the largest attendance increases in NCAA football history.

Sincerely,

Russ Potts

HRP/lw

MOST EFFECTIVE MARKETING PROMOTION FOR SEASON TICKETS:

As a new franchise in a geographical area (Central Texas) eager for professional baseball, the marketing of season tickets was a two-year process that consisted primarily of getting out into the community and introducing the Round Rock Express to the people of the area. We realized that it was our responsibility to become a community "partner" and get involved in as many community events as possible if we expected the community to respond in kind. Our marketing slogan was "Express Yourself" and fortunately, many fans did! Three months prior to our season opening game, we cut off season ticket sales at 4,500 in order to accommodate single-game ticket buyers (our stadium seats 8,000). We also offered a "Friday Fireworks Package" which included 11 games and we sold 2,500 of those. This response was very encouraging for a new franchise, and it was also a plus that the Round Rock/Austin area is a very sports-minded community.

TWO MOST SUCCESSFUL SINGLE GAME PROMOTIONS:

1. "Friday Night Fireworks" – the Express staged a fireworks show following every Friday home game, plus Opening Night, Fourth of July and our final home game – Fan Appreciation Night. An average show was 10-12 minutes in duration, with a 15-18 minute program for the "special" nights. We asked our fireworks company to continue to be creative with their presentations, and each show had a "theme" with specially prepared music. Our fans – as well as our sponsor – were very pleased and each Friday game was a sellout.

2. "Used Car Night" – sponsored by a local automobile dealer, we had the opportunity to give away seven used cars during a game. Fans (age 18 and older with valid Texas drivers license, current insurance, etc.) were handed a registration form as they entered the ballpark and during selected inning breaks, the vehicles were driven onto the field to specific music ("Mustang Sally"....."Pick-Up Man"....."Low Rider"......etc.) and a description was read on each. As the vehicle was driven off the field, the winning name was drawn and announced. It was a fun evening, and provided a refreshing change to our regular game presentation.

MARKETING TOOLS TO ATTRACT MORE STUDENTS TO GAMES:

Selected games were designated as "College Nights" where students with current college ID could get half-price tickets. These dates were held in conjunction with our Half-Price Group Nights that were scheduled for weeknights. Also, our Thursday night games featured live music before and after the games that seemed to attract young adult fans as well.

THOUGHT FOR PROMOTING THE 2001 SEASON:

While the Round Rock Express has enjoyed a very successful Inaugural Season with record attendance and great public response, our organization is aware that aggressive and creative marketing is the key to sustaining that level of success. We are satisfied with our results, but careful not to become complacent. Planning began in August for our 2001 promotional schedule, which will include the most popular ideas from the 2000 season, as well as new promotions and projects that will keep our fans interested during the off-season and our "sophomore" season.

Thank you for inviting the Round Rock Express to participate in this project.

Sincerely,

Jay Miller

Jay Miller
Vice-President/General Manager
Round Rock Express Baseball Club
E-mail address: jmiller@roundrockexpress.com

February 7, 2001

Bill Foster
Special Assistant to the Commissioner
WAC
Box 2329
Coppell, TX 75109-8329

Dear Bill:

Please accept my apologies for us taking this amount of time to get back to you.

Per your request, here is the following information you requested from the organization:

1. **Our most effective marketing program for season ticket sales.**

    - Asking our sales staff to make 40 new dials a day, 10 appointments a week and making ticket recommendations on customers needs.
    - Marketing all brands during all events at ARCO Arena. "Fish where the Fish are".

2. **Your two most successful single game promotions?**

    - Partnership with McDonald's that offer discounted tickets, basketball and coupons for free food.
    - Partnership with local grocery chain with similar promotion as McDonald's.

3. **Your two most successful marketing tools to get more students to attend games?**

    - Setting appointments with local schools and asking them what their needs are, then making recommendations.
    - Offering a group ticket discount to all members of organization.

4. **One thought to better promote your 01-00 season that you did not do last season?**

    - Add value to investing. More benefits or free stuff!

5. **Any final thoughts regarding sports marketing?**

    - Always make sure you base any ticket recommendations on the customer's needs. We say, "what's in it for them"? They are investing in you, so make sure they know that you care about them.

I hope this helps you and if you have any questions, please let me know. Good luck!

Best regards,

Javier Zuniga
Assistant Director, Relationship Enhancement

From the SF CANARIES BASEBALL

1. Your most effective marketing promotion for season ticket sales?

    a. Handwritten individual notes to potentials.

    b. Radio commercials with the names of people who have signed up.

2. Your two most successful single game promotions.

    a. Tonya Harding mini-bat night

    b. Friday night fireworks

3. Your two most successful marketing tools to get more students to attend?
    a. Thirsty Thursdays ($1.00 beer/hot dog)
    b. Silly Theme Nights (Pet nights, etc.)

4. One thought to better promote your 2000-2001 season that you didn't do last season.
    a. Target senior citizens
    b. Target teenagers

5. Any final comments regarding your sports marketing?

    a. Take chances

    b. Have fun

    c. Love what you do

    d. Respect the integrity/history of your chosen sport.

Quakes 2000 Promotional Schedule

**Taken From The Rancho Cucamonga Quakes' terrific Game Program

April
- Sat. 8 — Fireworks **AT&T Wireless Services**
- Sun. 9 — CD Holders **Charter Communications**
- Fri. 14 — Magnetic Schedules **Frazee Paint**
- Fri. 21 — **Renaissance Pleasure Faire** Night: Pre-game show & free tickets
- Sat. 22 — Giveaway Item **San Diego Padres**
- Sun. 30 — Tremor's Birthday Party & Mascot Mania

May
- Fri. 5 — Water Bottles **Cucamonga County Water District**
- Sat. 6 — Yo-Yo's **Charter Communications**
- Fri. 19 — Fireworks **Edwards IMAX Theatres**
- Sat. 20 — Adult T-Shirts **Washington Mutual**
- Sun. 21 — Sports Hero Bob Boone Appearance **BIC & KOLA 99.9 FM**
- Mon. 22 — "Strike out Chemotherapy-Anemia" Night **Ortho Biotech**

June
- Thur. 1 — Army Appreciation Night **U.S. Army**
- Fri. 2 — Sports Bag **California Highway Patrol**
- Sat. 3 — Louisville Slugger Baseball Bats **PFF Bank & Trust**
- Sun. 4 — Autograph Books **AmeriSuites**
- Sat. 10 — Fireworks **Allcom**
- Fri. 23 — Jimmy Buffett Theme Night **KCAL 96.7 FM**
- Sat. 24 — Baseball Gloves **Snyder's of Hanover**
- Sun. 25 — Checkbook Covers **Bank of America**

July
- Tue. 4 — Fireworks **The Beer Hunter**
- Fri. 7 — Team Posters **CDF & USFS**
- Sat. 8 — Floppy Hats **Arrowhead Mtn. Spring Water**
- Sun. 9 — Scoreboard Clipboards **Used Oil Collection**
- Fri. 14 — Sport the Mascot Appearance **Charter Communications**
- Sat. 15 — Baseball Caps **The Home Depot**
- Sun. 16 — Seat Cushions **Inter Mountain Mortgage**
- Wed. 19 — Car Giveaway **Mark Christopher Oldsmobile**
- Fri. 21 — Mouse Pads **superpages.com**
- Sat. 22 — Harley-Davidson Theme Night **Pomona Valley Harley-Davidson**

August
- Fri. 4 — Fireworks **McDonald's**
- Sat. 5 — Team Photos **Red Roof Inns**
- Sun. 6 — Sports Hero Bobby Grich Appearance **BIC & KOLA 99.9 FM**
- Wed. 9 — Top Prospect Card Set **Greyhound**
- Thur. 17 — Rainforest Awareness Night **Rainforest Cafe**
- Fri. 18 — ZOOperstars Appearance **Charter Communications**
- Thur. 24 — Giveaway Item **San Diego Padres**
- Sun. 27 — Lunch Pails **Washington Mutual**

September
- Fri. 1 — Beanie Bears
- Sat. 2 — Fireworks **CAL FED BANK**

BRING IT HOME

Fun...Family...FAN-atics

SPORT the MASCOT
Friday, July 14

ZOOperstars
Friday, August 18

RANCHO CUCAMONGA QUAKES

THE UNIVERSITY OF TEXAS AT EL PASO

UTEP ATHLETICS
SEASON TICKET PROMOTION

FAMILY FUN PACK

Heading into the 1999 UTEP football season UTEP Athletics made a decision to lower ticket prices for the football season. At the same time UTEP Athletics created the Family Fun Pack. The Family Fun Pack is a season ticket promotion targeted toward families.

The Family Fun Pack included five season general admission tickets for the cost of $75.00. The season ticket package included two adult general admission tickets and three children general admission tickets along with a season parking pass. The ticket price for each of these tickets per game averaged out to be $3.00.

The Family Fun Pack season ticket package was located in the general admission seating located in the Sun Bowl in the North end zone of the stadium. The Family Fun Pack was a success, as we saw our overall season ticket base increase partly due to the Family Fun Pack. UTEP has also created a Family Fun Pack for men's basketball. The basketball Family Fun Pack was set at a cost of $270.00 and included two adult season tickets and three children season tickets in the upper rows of our basketball arena.

In 1999, attendance for UTEP football games increase by over 16,000 more fans per game then the previous years. The Family Fun Pack assisted in the increase of attendance.

FOR QUESTIONS ABOUT THE FAMILY FUN PACK CONTACT EITHER

ROB SESICH	*OR*	*JEFF RANK*
DIRECTOR OF MARKETING		*PROMOTIONS COORDINATOR*
UTEP ATHLETICS		*UTEP ATHLETICS*
(915) 747-5833		*(915) 747-6787*
rsesich@miners.utep.edu		*jrank@miners.utep.edu*

Fax: (915) 747-5444

Department of Intercollegiate Athletics

Marketing & Promotions

Brumbelow Bldg. Rm. 107
500 W. University Ave
El Paso, Texas
79968-0579
(915) 747-5347
FAX (915) 747-5444

THE UNIVERSITY OF TEXAS AT EL PASO

UTEP ATHLETICS SEASON TICKET PROMOTION

TEAM FUND DRIVE

One of the most successful season ticket promotion UTEP athletics conducted was the "Team Fund Drive". The team fund drive is a season ticket drive to generate new revenue with the assistance from volunteers.

Starting in early spring prior to the following athletic year, UTEP volunteers are formed into 10 teams of 8 to 15 people. Teams are organized similar to a professional sports league. There is a commissioner who oversees the entire league. Each team has a captain who coordinates their team of volunteers. Before the teams begin selling each team will attend a required training camp. The training camp familiarizes the teams with ticket information and overall general information about the UTEP athletic department. Goals are also set for the fund drive at the training camp.

Following training camp, teams attend a kick-off dinner to start the fund drive. Once the fund drive has started teams begin selling football, basketball and women's sports tickets by soliciting the El Paso community. Targeted audiences, data of who to solicit, former donor list and past season ticket holders are gathered by the volunteers with assistance from the UTEP athletic department. The entire fund drive runs for 4 weeks with an optional 5th week if needed.

Weekly meetings are held at popular restaurants to answer questions and to get updates and reports from the teams. Individual prizes like car flags, bumper stickers and mostly promotional items are given out at the weekly meetings to the teams who are leading in sales. At the end of the drive there is a final meeting where ending reports are gathered. More valuable prizes are then given out to the top teams. Prizes such as a trip to a future football away game, leather UTEP business bags and golf shirts are some example of prizes given away.

The program proved to be very successful with over $100,000 dollars in new money generated in the Spring of 2000. The structure of the program brought out competition between the teams which motivated the volunteers to sell more. Some adjustments will be made to the program, but the athletic department is looking forward to running the team fund drive in Spring 2001.

FOR QUESTIONS ABOUT THE TEAM FUND DRIVE PLEASE CONTACT

DARREN D'ATTILIO
ASSISTANT DIRECTOR FOR DEVELOPMENT
UTEP ATHLETICS
ddattilio@miners.utep.edu
(915) 747-8759
Fax: (915) 747-5444

Department of Intercollegiate Athletics

Marketing & Promotions

Brumbelow Bldg. Rm. 107
500 W. University Ave
El Paso, Texas
79968-0579
(915) 747-5347
FAX (915) 747-5444

THE UNIVERSITY OF TEXAS AT EL PASO

UTEP ATHLETICS STUDENT PROMOTION

ZOO CREW STUDENT BODY SPIRIT GROUP!

In the late fall of 1999, the UTEP Athletic Department created a student spirit group called "The Zoo Crew" sponsored by Little Caesar's Pizza. The goal was not only to increase more student involvement at basketball games, but at the same time increase student body attendance.

A designated section was made for the spirit group to sit in during the games. Each member received a membership card and a Zoo Crew tee-shirt. The membership card not only made sure they had a seat in the spirit section, but also allowed for 10% off any purchase made at Little Caesar's Pizza.

Members registered at spirit group meetings held at dorms and during basketball games. A formal meeting was held at a basketball practice where students were able to meet both men's and women's head coaches and players. At this formal meeting membership cards, Zoo Crew shirts and free pizza was also available to the students provided by Little Caesar's Pizza.

Right away a difference was recognized in the student section during games. The enthusiasm created at the games from the group not only gave inspiration to the players, but also created a great college basketball atmosphere.

FOR ANY QUESTIONS YOU MAY HAVE ABOUT THE ZOO CREW PLEASE CONTACT:

ROB SESICH OR *JEFF RANK*
DIRECTOR OF MARKETING   *PROMOTIONS COORDINATOR*
UTEP ATHLETICS   *UTEP ATHLETICS*
(915) 747-5833   *(915)-747-6787*
rsesich@miners.utep.edu   *jrank@miners.utep.edu*

Fax: (915) 747-5444

Department of Intercollegiate Athletics

Marketing & Promotions

Brumbelow Bldg. Rm. 107
500 W. University Ave
El Paso, Texas
79968-0579
(915) 747-5347
FAX (915) 747-5444

THE UNIVERSITY OF TEXAS AT EL PASO

UTEP ATHLETICS PROMOTION FOR FOOTBALL

FURR'S MINER TOWN AND THE EL PASO TIMES FUN ZONE

Furr's Miner Town

During the 1999 football season UTEP Athletics reintroduced a tailgating venue held before each home UTEP football game. The name of the tailgating venue is "The Furr's Miner Town". Furr's Miner Town was moved from the football practice field which was away from the stadium and into the parking lot right in front of the busiest entrance to the Sun Bowl.

Furr's Miner Town had everything a fan could want in a pre-game tailgate area. There were inflatable rides for fans to jump around on including a giant slide, concession booths, UTEP merchandise was on sale, a beer garden and a live band played at every tailgate party. To make sure fans would not miss any action of other college football games being played across the country, a television tent area was set up covering those games.

As part of their total sponsorship package with UTEP Athletics, Furr's Supermarkets agreed to sponsor the tailgate area all season long. Fans were able to use their Furr's discount frequent shopper card to receive a "Furr's Family Food Pack" for a dollar off the regular price.

El Paso Times Fun Zone

Also during the 1999 football season, UTEP Athletics introduced a new entertainment area targeted towards families. To allow for parents to watch the game and feel safe for their child to go into a supervised area to play, UTEP Athletics created "The El Paso Times Fun Zone".

Sponsored by the local newspaper, the Fun Zone featured inflatable rides, face painting, sumo wrestling, Warner Brothers characters walking around and a balloon artist to entertain children. The Fun Zone was open three hours prior to kick-off and was shut down at the end of the third quarter. The Fun Zone was supervised by a local security staff hired for UTEP football games.

The overall success of the El Paso Times Fun Zone has encouraged the athletics department to possibly expand the area and add more entertainment next season.

FOR QUESTIONS YOU MAY HAVE CONCERNING THE FURR'S MINER TOWN OR THE EL PASO TIMES FUN ZONE PLEASE CONTACT:

ROB SESICH   *OR*   *JEFF RANK*
DIRECTOR OF MARKETING   *PROMOTIONS COORDINATOR*
UTEP ATHLETICS   *UTEP ATHLETICS*
(915) 747-5833   *(915) 747-6787*
rsesich@miners.utep.edu   *jrank@miners.utep.edu*

Fax: (915) 747-5444

Department of Intercollegiate Athletics

Marketing & Promotions

Brumbelow Bldg. Rm. 107
500 W. University Ave
El Paso, Texas
79968-0579
(915) 747-5347
FAX (915) 747-5444

THE UNIVERSITY OF TEXAS AT EL PASO

UTEP ATHLETICS STUDENT PROMOTION

ZOO CREW STUDENT BODY SPIRIT GROUP!

In the late fall of 1999, the UTEP Athletic Department created a student spirit group called "The Zoo Crew" sponsored by Little Caesar's Pizza. The goal was not only to increase more student involvement at basketball games, but at the same time increase student body attendance.

A designated section was made for the spirit group to sit in during the games. Each member received a membership card and a Zoo Crew tee-shirt. The membership card not only made sure they had a seat in the spirit section, but also allowed for 10% off any purchase made at Little Caesar's Pizza.

Members registered at spirit group meetings held at dorms and during basketball games. A formal meeting was held at a basketball practice where students were able to meet both men's and women's head coaches and players. At this formal meeting membership cards, Zoo Crew shirts and free pizza was also available to the students provided by Little Caesar's Pizza.

Right away a difference was recognized in the student section during games. The enthusiasm created at the games from the group not only gave inspiration to the players, but also created a great college basketball atmosphere.

FOR ANY QUESTIONS YOU MAY HAVE ABOUT THE ZOO CREW PLEASE CONTACT:

ROB SESICH
DIRECTOR OF MARKETING
UTEP ATHLETICS
(915) 747-5833
rsesich@miners.utep.edu

OR

JEFF RANK
PROMOTIONS COORDINATOR
UTEP ATHLETICS
(915)-747-6787
jrank@miners.utep.edu

Fax: (915) 747-5444

Department of Intercollegiate Athletics

Marketing & Promotions

Brumbelow Bldg. Rm. 107
500 W. University Ave
El Paso, Texas
79968-0579
(915) 747-5347
FAX (915) 747-5444

THE UNIVERSITY OF TEXAS AT EL PASO

UTEP ATHLETICS
PROMOTION FOR FOOTBALL

*FURR'S MINER TOWN AND THE
EL PASO TIMES FUN ZONE*

Furr's Miner Town

During the 1999 football season UTEP Athletics reintroduced a tailgating venue held before each home UTEP football game. The name of the tailgating venue is "The Furr's Miner Town". Furr's Miner Town was moved from the football practice field which was away from the stadium and into the parking lot right in front of the busiest entrance to the Sun Bowl.

Furr's Miner Town had everything a fan could want in a pre-game tailgate area. There were inflatable rides for fans to jump around on including a giant slide, concession booths, UTEP merchandise was on sale, a beer garden and a live band played at every tailgate party. To make sure fans would not miss any action of other college football games being played across the country, a television tent area was set up covering those games.

As part of their total sponsorship package with UTEP Athletics, Furr's Supermarkets agreed to sponsor the tailgate area all season long. Fans were able to use their Furr's discount frequent shopper card to receive a "Furr's Family Food Pack" for a dollar off the regular price.

El Paso Times Fun Zone

Also during the 1999 football season, UTEP Athletics introduced a new entertainment area targeted towards families. To allow for parents to watch the game and feel safe for their child to go into a supervised area to play, UTEP Athletics created "The El Paso Times Fun Zone".

Sponsored by the local newspaper, the Fun Zone featured inflatable rides, face painting, sumo wrestling, Warner Brothers characters walking around and a balloon artist to entertain children. The Fun Zone was open three hours prior to kick-off and was shut down at the end of the third quarter. The Fun Zone was supervised by a local security staff hired for UTEP football games.

The overall success of the El Paso Times Fun Zone has encouraged the athletics department to possibly expand the area and add more entertainment next season.

FOR QUESTIONS YOU MAY HAVE CONCERNING THE FURR'S MINER TOWN OR THE EL PASO TIMES FUN ZONE PLEASE CONTACT:

ROB SESICH	OR	*JEFF RANK*
DIRECTOR OF MARKETING		*PROMOTIONS COORDINATOR*
UTEP ATHLETICS		*UTEP ATHLETICS*
(915) 747-5833		*(915) 747-6787*
rsesich@miners.utep.edu		*jrank@miners.utep.edu*

Fax: (915) 747-5444

*Department of
Intercollegiate
Athletics*

*Marketing &
Promotions*

Brumbelow Bldg. Rm. 107
500 W. University Ave
El Paso, Texas
79968-0579
(915) 747-5347
FAX (915) 747-5444

THE UNIVERSITY OF TEXAS AT EL PASO

UTEP ATHLETICS BEST SINGLE NIGHT PROMOTION

VOLKSWAGEN BUG GIVE AWAY

In the 1999 UTEP football season at a home football game we gave away a Volkswagen Bug to a lucky fan. The promotion was sponsored by a local corporation, a Volkswagen dealership and a radio station.

The promotion started in the Summer months and ended at the half-time of the football game sponsored by the three game sponsors. To have a chance at winning the car, fans were able to register their names at the radio station's live remotes and the Volkswagen dealership throughout the Summer.

A total of six contestants were chosen to participate in the contest at the game. Four of the finalist were chosen from registration at the live remotes held prior to the game and two were chosen at the game. During the half-time of the sponsored football game the car was brought out to the fifty yard line to be given away. Each of the six finalists were given a car key. The finalist with the car key that started the car, won the car.

FOR ANY QUESTIONS CONCERNING THIS PROMOTION CONTACT:

ROB SESICH   *OR*   *JEFF RANK*
DIRECTOR OF MARKETING   *PROMOTIONS COORDINATOR*
UTEP ATHLETICS   *UTEP ATHLETICS*
(915) 747-5833   *(915) 747-6787*
rsesich@miners.utep.edu   *jrank@miners.utep.edu*

Fax: (915) 747-5444

Department of Intercollegiate Athletics

Marketing & Promotions

Brumbelow Bldg. Rm. 107
500 W. University Ave
El Paso, Texas
79968-0579
(915) 747-5347
FAX (915) 747-5444

THE UNIVERSITY OF TEXAS AT EL PASO

UTEP MINERS

One thought to better promote your upcoming season.

Increase the visibility of the athletic programs and upcoming seasons through newspaper advertising, radio advertising, billboards and television.

Final comments in regards to sports marketing
It is very important to know who your fans are and what their likes and dislikes are. Getting fans to an event is one task, but getting those fans to come back to more events is even a bigger task. Sports marketers should ask how is the customer's experience when he or she comes to the event? How is parking? How are the concessions? Are the in game promotions entertaining? Most importantly try your best in making the fans game day experience a enjoyable one.

Department of Intercollegiate Athletics

Marketing & Promotions

Brumbelow Bldg. Rm. 107
500 W. University Ave
El Paso, Texas
79968-0579
(915) 747-5347
FAX (915) 747-5444

INTERCOLLEGIATE ATHLETICS FOR WOMEN
THE UNIVERSITY OF TEXAS AT AUSTIN

Bellmont Hall 324 • Austin, Texas 78712 • (512) 471-7693 • FAX: (512) 471-3985

Your most effective marketing promotion for season ticket sales? List top two.
1. Mail season ticket brochures to foundation donors within 50 mile radius.
2. Solicit holders of season tickets in sports apart from the one being sold.

Your two most successful single game promotions (in terms of ticket sale response):
1. Area youth nights for youth teams in specific sport.
2. Heavy promotions of top flight competition with national caliber teams in their respective sports.

Your two most successful marketing tools to get more students to attend games?
1. Combined sports package which offers season ticket to all sports at one low price.
2. Competitive attendance incentives between campus groups.

One thought to better promote your 2000-2001 season that you didn't do last season (colleges, pick a sport):
Women's Basketball--Conference wide promotion to attract 1 million fans to conference games and lead the nation in conference attendance.

Jerry Johnson
Assistant Athletic Director
  for Administration and Marketing
Intercollegiate Athletics for Women
(512) 232-2360 (voice)
(512) 471-2177 (fax)
jjohnson@athletics.utexas.edu

NOTES

CHAPTER 13
ANALYZE — ANALYZE — ANALYZE

As we've mentioned throughout the book, there are so many very important phases of your job. Not only the creative thinking, having an exciting product, a championship team, your organization, your people skills and enthusiastic approach — it all goes together in one big package.

To be successful, and to make sure you hit a home run with every aspect of your marketing and selling, you need to occasionally slow down and ANALYZE what you are doing and what you've done and what you're going to be doing. Each phase individually has to be beneficial for the time, money and effort you are expending. If it isn't, you have to either tweak it, and look for more success, and the hardest part, is maybe you have to scrap it and move into another direction. The latter is unfortunate but sometimes necessary. It's difficult to bat 1,000 in every single idea/effort that you do. You have to plow ahead but with educated "guesstimates" of what will be successful for you. Ditto for sales; keep the head up and be confident that your particular ideas and effort will work. You can't get your head down. You as the leader have to have supreme confidence in what you are doing. You may need discussions with your staff and/or with others in your field, to get some different input and/or encouragement.

As a head coach in basketball for 39 years, I often did speaking on motivation. Our need as the head coach, was to motivate our team, our staff, our fans, and the media – a pretty tall assignment. Now who would motivate me? Who motivates the motivator? This is basically the same situation. You have to have confidence in yourself and your ability, faith in what you are doing, and be able to push the right buttons to make things work out and be successful. Self motivation becomes the answer to the above question.

I think some kind of an advisory board or something similar could be a big help. It would have to be a board that you would put together – one that you would have confidence in, and one that would be willing to keep your areas of discussion confidential. Possibly more eyes and ears can keep you better posted and also help with the "idea machine".

When you analyze, how is this done? I believe there are several methods that can be utilized. One is through your regular staff meetings. You discuss with your staff what is working and what is not. If you have an assistant that works closely with you, discuss the same with that person. However, with you, the leader, you must be ready for suggestions and ideas to create a successful situation.

Another possibility is through your friends in the same job situation as you, but possibly not in your same league and not your competition. We've mentioned about developing a group of people outside your area that you might "network with" and be able to discuss on the phone your situation/problems and the like. You have to trust these people and keep your problems completely confidential.

Actually, ANALYZE — ANALYZE — ANALYZE, says it all. Whenever you can, wherever you can, you need to look back and reflect and see where it might have been done better. Then you have a mission statement and a set of objectives, it's your responsibility to meet these. If you are "managing by walking around" – keep your eyes and ears open. Be sure you see areas that you can improve and hear from those you trust who might

> **EXCEL at customer service, convenience for the customer, and surround yourself with smiling faces.**

offer constructive suggestions for improvement. EXCEL at customer service, convenience for the customer, and surround yourself with smiling faces.

When you are creating your marketing campaign and are looking for key statements and points of emphasis that will SELL for you, much is made in business about U.S.P. ... that means UNIQUE SELLING PROPOSITION. This can, and should be, applied to what you are doing. In the creation of your ticket flyers, U.S.P. can be, and should be, a factor in your campaign. What is it that's UNIQUE about your team? Your school? The upcoming season? Can we get beyond just the word exciting? Will there be a lot of scoring, hard-nosed defense, more touchdowns per game? You have a terrific arena. Break that down into its individual parts: you've got convenient parking, easy access to concessions, helpful ushers to direct you to your seat, entertaining team, one that could lead the nation in scoring, watch the excitement of your great three-point shooters, etc. Why buy a season ticket to your games? What are the benefits? So much in marketing in brochures are thrown out in generalities, so dig deep and come up with some <u>unique specifics</u> of the upcoming season. Consider this when you are putting together your sales pitch. You can be different and fan friendly by being the only school in your conference with preferred parking for the season ticket holders and personal food/beverage service at your seat in a special section, or front row seating. Unfortunately, we can't offer guarantees like different products we use, but some schools have tried this with mixed results.

Depending upon the type of school where you are working, much in the way of market research and different studies can be made. If you are working for a college or university, and particularly if there is a strong business department, you can get research projects completed for you as class projects.

YOU ARE THE ARCHITECT of your program. Your objectives and ideas reflect the direction and timetable you will use. Remember, "PROGRESS USUALLY BRINGS SOME COMPLAINTS" — if you are really doing a good job of increasing attendance, interest and revenue, not everybody will be happy. Remember, "you can't please all the people, all of the time". With increased attendance, people will find that your arena/stadium will be a little more crowded and some inconveniences will be incurred – no matter how well you're prepared. Parking will be a little more crowded and going to the concessions stands will take a little longer. Some of these problems will come about naturally because of your marketing. You have to be able to accept some criticism and accept it as being constructive and helpful. You can't dwell on the negative for more than about two seconds.

YOU ARE THE ARCHITECT of your program.

"PROGRESS USUALLY BRINGS SOME COMPLAINTS"

> **Some people were born to complain while others have perfected that skill through the years.**

Some people were born to complain while others have perfected that skill through the years. YOU must be careful in all your efforts to use good judgment, conduct yourself and your events with CLASS, and always maintain that upbeat, energetic, and enthusiastic manner. You're the leader and you are the one that sets the pace.

Complicating matters are the apparent high interest of fans in the bizarre and different – witness the now defunct XFL pro football and the pro wrestling. Lots of interest and high energy stuff – show time. Do it right and work at your "one fan at a time". Times have changed, BUT THE FORMULA FOR SUCCESS HASN'T. It's still the basics. Ask any coach who loses two games in a row, and they'll all say they're going to return to the basics; the fundamentals.

> **Times have changed, BUT THE FORMULA FOR SUCCESS HASN'T. It's still the basics.**

So it's necessary to walk a fine line (maybe the old adage, "when in doubt – don't" comes in to play), ANALYZE what you are doing and is it successful according to your game plan? If YOU feel it's working and attendance is increasing, fan interest is up, and you've improved the revenue stream, and you've done it with CLASS. GO FOR IT.

You do have to have your "eyes and ears" alert at all times to what the fans want from your event. You can't give them everything, but you usually can "fix" some of the smaller stuff. You CAN LEARN from those who are coming to the games on a regular basis. They look at their experience a little bit differently than you do.

We haven't purposely ignored the junior high school. Practically everything that we talked about in this book can be applicable to a junior high school situation. The exception is that many do not charge for any of their contests. However, you can certainly work at building more interest in the various sports. The fan interest, when you build at the lower grades, has a definite carry-over effect to the high school. So just as you build a solid program at the high school level, one fan at a time, you can do the same with the junior high. If you don't charge currently, and you feel that the additional income would really help, you might do a "watered down" ticket price. You might only charge $2.00 per game or have a season ticket for just $10.00 – or a family pass for $25.00. Study this, it might be worth it as your programs cost money too and those costs are increasing. Study the possibilities that you might have, carefully. You will incur costs for ticket takers, printing of tickets (although this can be a trade-out), and you could raise your revenue base up slowly. The same could be said with attempting to take a non-revenue sport into the next level; that of becoming a revenue sport. More schools are looking at this possibility to raise more money and slow down some of the expenses of the various sports.

> **The fan interest, when you build at the lower grades, has a definite carry-over effect to the high school.**

NOTES

CHAPTER 14

FUTURE IDEAS —

WHERE DO WE GET THEM?

As with any profession, improvement and ideas can come from many sources. One is to attend seminars and workshops. Some are pricey but pick your spots. Many of these can be very helpful to your job and your career. The networking alone can make them beneficial. Be sure to take along plenty of your business cards to exchange with your new friends. If the price is too high, perhaps you can purchase the audio tapes of the conference. These are great for your car. This is another reason why you should be involved in some fund raising for your budget. Perhaps, that would allow you to take in a seminar or two utilizing this source for expenses. On something like this, you need extra permission and documentation to handle the finances. The pro sports have some excellent seminars and information. That might be difficult to get notes from this source but having a friend who is attending, you could get ideas. I personally have enjoyed the big Nataional Premium Show in Dallas in early January each year. You need a special pass for this. A manufacture's rep might help you gain access; BUT what a way to spend a day. You need about a full day to get through all the rows of new products that are exhibited.

E.J. Krause & Associates, Inc.

6550 Rock Spring Drive–Suite 500

Bethesda, MD 20817

Tel. (301) 493-5500

They conduct an international sport summit trade show and conference as well as produce a "Who's Who In The Sports Industry" Directory. They had audio tapes of their January 2001 for sale at $300.00 for the complete set.

Jon Spoelstra S.R.O Partners 1314 N. W. Irving Suite 408 Portland, OR 97209 Phone: (503) 297-2332 Fax: (503) 241-5023	Anything written by Jon Spoelstra (i.e. "How To Sell The Last Seat In The House"), with much pro experience with the Portland Trailblazers and the New Jersey Nets; and much more, is worth the money.
Bill Veeck Promotional Seminar Contact Mike Veeck P.O. Box 20819 Charleston, SC 29413	This has been highly recommended to me by several sources. Excellent staff -- I hope to attend this year.
Sports Summit 2002 E.J. Crause & Assoc. 6550 Rock Spring Drive Suite 500 Bethesda, MD 20817-1126	High level conference and exhibition.
Facility Revenue Forum 636 Northland Blvd. Suite 250 Cincinnati, OH 45240 (513) 674-0550	The Second Annual Facility Revenue Fourm to be held in June/July in San Francisco.
IQPC 150 Clove Road P.O. Box 401 Little Falls, NJ 07424-0421	This is an Internet ticketing seminar with speakers on opeations/management of box offices, ticket sales, e-commerce, paperless ticketing system, etc.
Dan Kennedy Kennedy Inner Circle, Inc. 5818 N. 7th St. #103 Phoenix, AZ 85014 (602) 977-7707 Fax (602) 269-3113 Website: www.dankennedy.com	Absolutely the best in direct marketing; has all sorts of books, audio tapes, seminars, newsletter, speaker. Anything is terrific by Dan. Dan is a "marketing machine" – nonstop.
Richard Alm Dallas Morning News Dallas, Texas	Excellent column every Saturday in The Dallas Morning News, in the Business Section. Outstanding features on the latest on the business side of sports.
Team Marketing Report, Inc. 660 W. Grand Ave. Suite 100E Chicago, IL 60610 (312) 829-7060	Very fine monthly publication; Sponsor FactBook, Disk, Promotion Ideas & up-to-date marketing report monthly (one-year subscription $195).

E-mail networking gives you great ideas that you can possibly adapt to your own situation. If it doesn't exactly fit for you, you might be able to give it a slightly different twist so it would work. I would definitely develop an e-mail NETWORK with your friends at other schools working in the same capacity as you. E-mail might be the easiest of all methods to keep in touch and exchange ideas and less expensive than telephone and fax and more convenient. If a group of sports marketing people from a close-by geographic area would get together on a Saturday morning for an in-person seminar to exchange ideas, this could be beneficial. However, close by might mean that your opponents might not share as much as those from a distance. Any in-person get together, don't forget your notebook and pen to write your notes. If you are sitting at the computer with your new e-mail friends, this is an excellent time to take notes or print and put in that file.

Anytime you spend money to get together with a group of your sports marketing people— IT'S AN INVESTMENT IN YOUR FUTURE.

Anytime you spend money to get together with a group of your sports marketing people—IT'S AN INVESTMENT IN YOUR FUTURE. It's the same with the investment of your time—it's an investment in your future.

If you are trying to attend a seminar or purchase audio or video tapes on subjects that might help improve your operation, you can try to get your school to pay for it. You need to write up a proposal giving the date and time of the seminar, include a copy of the brochure, how it will help you and the school, and approximate total cost. Emphasize the benefits to the school and your program...and keep your finges crossed for approval.

Try to tie-in with a MENTOR – someone who would be a good influence in your career. This person could be a big help to you educationally and also with networking and moving up the career ladder.

What do you know this week that you didn't know last week? "Anything green–grows." Life is a continuing education–ditto for sports marketing personnel. The library is a "do it yourself" education."

Magazines and newspapers give you lots of inspiration and source materials. I saved an article on fund-raising (capital campaign types) that was excellent; it came from the June 1997 issue of Kiplinger's Personal Finance Magazine. I received an issue of "Business Bottom Line" – right there on the front page was a feature article by Jay Levinson, Guerilla Marketing International, entitled: "How To Out-Market The Big Guys Without Their Big Bucks" – it was not specifically about sports but much of it applied to what you do. Magazines like Fortune, Forbes, Entrepreneur, Inc., 2.0 Business, Money Magazine, Success, etc. will have articles that can apply to your work.

The specific magazines on sports like Sports Illustrated, football magazines, Sporting News, Baseball Digest, Basketball America, and others will have articles that can fit your job.

COLLEGES

CAMPUS INSIDER
By Dick Patrick

Creativity attracts sponsorships

Companies pay to get on campus

Colleges and corporations are becoming creative in their use of perks in multimillion-dollar sponsorships.

At Maryland, Comcast is paying $20 million over 10 years for naming rights to a new arena. The company also is wiring all dorm rooms for cable TV.

Michigan landed a three-year, $1.8 million deal with Bank One, which gets to install ATMs in advertising-free Michigan Stadium, according to *The Detroit News*.

MBNA America Bank gave $300,000 in royalties last year and gets information such as addresses and phone numbers for season ticketholders, booster-club members and donors to the athletic department.

The big prize for the biggest donors: four expenses-paid trips on the team charter and at the team hotel for the Orange Bowl earlier this month. Similar packages are offered for the next two years.

Michigan has 71 corporate sponsors paying $4.9 million, according to the Detroit paper.

The largest deal is with Nike, which offers $590,000 in payments, $930,000 in products plus $50,000 in scholarships and four internships, with preference given to minorities.

NOTES

CHAPTER 15
AUTHOR'S WRAP-UP, SOME CREDITS, AND SOME ADDED THOUGHTS FOR YOUR COFFEE BREAK

As we wrap things up, I would like to offer you the opportunity to send me a note — hopefully this material has been and will be helpful. As we started with the Introduction and Chapter One, we wanted to throw out ideas and suggestions that would benefit every reader. As we wrote this primarily for high schools, junior colleges and four-year colleges/universities, this is a wide gap. I've personally witnessed a disturbing trend. We are facing a fairly rapid decline in attendance at our games. With drop-offs in attendance, rising costs, and budget cuts, we need to be working harder at fixing this problem. Some of you have programs that are in full gear while others are just getting started. Some of our information may be too elementary for some and maybe impossible for others. We will be reaching a broad audience with a wide range of budgets, size of arenas/stadiums/gyms, number of sports expected to generate income, size of staff, and range of interest and expectation levels. I wish you the very best. This is an exciting profession, one where you can have a great future filled with opportunity and rewards.

I did want to list some of the early, in my mind, influences that got me more and more interested in the promotion and marketing end of sports, while I was still coaching. First, was NECESSITY, going from Rutgers University who at that time had a less than 3,000 seat arena to the University of Utah's 15,000 seat special events center. At the same time, the Utah Stars had just won the ABA Championship. They were a terrific team and organization. The University of Utah was and is, rich in tradition in basketball. I didn't have to be a genius to figure out we had a big problem, particularly with one starter returning. So, it was "roll up the sleeves" time. I hope I don't miss any, but these people I came in contact with either personally or through reading and they made a real impact with me:

BUD DUDLEY: Bud was at Villanova University at the time and later headed – the Liberty Bowl. I attended my first college football game courtesy of Bud's Grocery Bowl ticket opportunity. To get a free ticket to the football game between Villanova and the University of Georgia (game in Philadelphia), all you needed to do was buy $10 worth of groceries. I took advantage of that. Bud had a lot of promotions in those days.

BILL VEECK: Bill was the idol of all. I loved to read anything I could get my hands on regarding Bill Veeck's exploits and promotions. I was so pleased when I had an opportunity to talk to his son, Mike, who is a Chip off the old block, and he sent me terrific information for this book. Bill Veeck was and still is, THE inspiration for so many in this exciting field. I would highly recommend "MARKETING YOUR DREAMS, Business and Life Lessons from Bill Veeck,

Baseball's Marketing Genius" by Pat Williams (www.SportsPublishingInc.com.) It is great reading.

PAT WILLIAMS: On the cover of the above book, from Larry King: "Bi11 Veeck and Pat Williams ... what a winning exacta this is'.'" That kind of says it all. And Rudy Martzke's : "When it comes to marketing, no one's more qualified to document Bill Veeck's accomplishment than Pat Williams, the Bill Veeck of minor league baseball and pro basketball." Being in basketball, I closely watched all of Pat's travels through pro basketball and now with the Orlando Magic. What an idea guy, and a prolific writer.

RUSS POTTS: I first met Russ when he was in administration at the University of Maryland, and watched his promotions at Southern Methodist University with his famous, "Mustang Mania" – I really appreciated his contribution to this book in Chapter 12. Russ is still promoting – doing TV games in basketball. To my knowledge, he was the first sports marketer in college athletics. Russ is a real worker and thinker.

DON CANHAM: Talk about marketing; 102,000 seats occupied (sold) just about every other Saturday in the Fall, in Ann Arbor, Michigan. 1 don't know how many years ago, but Sports Illustrated did about eight or nine page story on him titled: "No Death For A Salesman" by Frank Deford. He was the athletic director at the University of Michigan. A great story. Don had great vision.

I was always fascinated with college press guides. Now high schools put out some outstanding pre-season material and the colleges have expanded their horizons. They've become recruiting books. My early recollection of schools that did a terrific job with these were Clemson University and the University of Iowa as well as the University of South Carolina. One of the early college coaches that did a lot of promotions, was George Raveling, when he was at Washington State University.

I've jokingly said that the motto of the sports marketing guru is: "It matters not whether we won or lost but how many PAID to see the game." I actually had an artist do the printing of this in the 60s when I coached at Rutgers University, and presented it to our Business Manager of Athletics at that time, Otto Hill, at our basketball banquet. It just occurred to me that with the trend today with so many more people WORKING AT HOME, that a new marketing approach might be geared to them; something like "get out of the house and into the main stream to see the Pony's play" or "get out and about" and some play on increasing your social life.

What you are doing is not easy. It's work and long hours. Never a dull minute; interesting and varied; no two days the same —keep utilizing those people skills and have fun.

GO GET EM' — the best of luck. Bring in those $$$$$$$$ and fill/sell those seats.

Bill Foster

SOME ADDED THOUGHTS

for Your Coffee Break ... and very important

1. You're involved with "No Quit Marketing".

2. NEED to stay focused all the time; just as the teams need to follow their game plan to be successful – so do YOU.

3. Don't ever stop your CREATIVITY.

4. Do what you do best – hire others to do the rest. Instead of "hire" – possibly delegate OR get a volunteer with expertise to handle if low or no staff money available.

   > **Do what you do best – hire others to do the rest.**

5. For your student intern program – hopefully you'll have enough interest (and you have to create and sell this) – that you'll be able to basically have "TRY-OUTS" like your athletic teams in order to get the best for your TEAM.

6. You don't have to be good to start -but you have to start to be good; very good and then you'll be rolling.

   > **You don't have to be good to start -but you have to start to be good; very good and then you'll be rolling.**

7. Set aside some time each week to "brainstorm" – analyze what you did; and what will WORK in the future – and work better.

8. You can be a copycat — don't waste a lot of time trying to come up with something totally new. You can "borrow".

9. Read–Read–Read; either through your library, book stores, etc. – you'll get some great IDEAS; maybe not immediately or from a direct source, but indirectly. Or with a little tinkering and adjusting to fit your school, it will WORK. That helps to develop your own creativity.

10. Utilizing some coaching theories — "I'd rather be over rehearsed than ambushed" – ditto for you and your TEAM.

11. Don't underestimate the importance of GAME MANAGEMENT — it's a strong part of your being fan friendly and indicates a smooth operation going on the day/night of your game.

12. Devote time to put together your operations manual and your responsibility assignments – then carefully "over-see".

13. During your brainstorming sessions – devote a time to CREATING IDEAS to get FREE FAVORABLE PUBLICITY for your teams. DITTO to get favorable free publicity for your PLAYERS.

14. If you don't have money available for advertising – CREATE EVENTS that will get you free publicity – involve CELEBRITIES – or have a clinic for players; clinics in football for women always get a lot of attention. HOWEVER, PLAN TO SUCCEED in these – you can't afford poor attendance – make sure you've got a definite number

attending that will give you a good start. In an area with just mediocre INTEREST, you may have to STAGE" these events so you have sufficient people attending- ALSO HAVE YOUR PHOTOGRAPHER there.

15. Remember you are ALWAYS BUILDING RELATIONSHIPS – it's easier to go back and SELL those people that have done business with you and are completely satisfied and ENJOY working with you. Re-selling to satisfied customers is easier than trying to find NEW customers — however you can never stop looking for new prospects.

16. Develop and keep fresh material on your Website and in your Newsletters. Don't underestimate the power of direct mail and keeping in touch and your keeping your valuable customers informed.

17. Know when to "pinch pennies" — your handling of finances is a MOST important part of your job. Keep accurate records and stay on top of all financial matters.

18. A fund raiser or two might be needed to increase the projects you feel are needed. Try to tie in with the MEDIA and also your advertisers or business partners.

19. Celebrity – has value.

20. The press can generate more business for you – make sure you have the best relations with them – take to lunch, breakfast – but just terrific P.R. with this type of informal get-together. When you do, make sure you have some "inside" news for them.

21. We have to remember that the provocative sells – the unusual – unfortunately coaches are not nuts about this aspect and probably ditto for the schools; SO BE CAREFUL AND USE YOUR HEAD on this one. It's most unfortunate that the OUTRAGEOUS creates much more interest and the media enjoys this. Talk radio needs callers – SO, to keep interest and gain listeners and callers, they must create "talk" that will add to their popularity.

    HOWEVER, you must, as a representative of a school, do things with CLASS – so pick and choose your ideas with this in mind. It only takes ONE CASE OF POOR JUDGMENT AND YOU COULD BE IN DEEP TROUBLE. You'd get publicity alright – but not the favorable kind.

"Identify your problems before you try to solve them".

22. "Identify your problems before you try to solve them".

23. Selling tickets is at the center of sports marketing – that's what it's all about. However, everything else surrounding it is a very important part of the end result.

24. Don't be afraid to walk around your arena/stadium when its empty and also when its game day/night much can be gained by observation each time you do so.

25. Your conference race will also dictate some different kind of promotional activities.

26. Review your marketing plan from time to time. This is your blueprint for success.

27. With all those season tickets and other promos you have working, you don't have to worry too much about poor weather or the team not playing well. You've got those seats sold in advance. Your dream is the same as the coach, win every game and play in an exciting fashion.

28. Sellouts drive ticket sales. And for that first sell-out, make sure your photographer is working overtime as well as your video coordinator. You also should be happy to alert the media about this event. It has to be a thrill and a half. Those photos will be used the following year in practically every flyer/brochure you produce.

29. When you take that walk around your arena/stadium, and you're doing fairly well at the gate, is there any room for a few low-cost

luxury boxes? These sell well and you usually can get sponsors to help with the finances and you can sell naming rights.

30. Always carefully check those concessions. Are they pulling in enough revenue? Are they fast, courteous, and efficient or are there long lines? How are the prices? Hopefully they are fair and profitable.

31. Create vanity phone numbers if you can; dial 1-800-Go Colts. or anything catchy and appealing to the fans.

32. Once things are rolling for you and even as attendance picks up, it's time to look at your MERCHANDISING PROGRAM. This can go as big as the need will be. If the team wins a championship, get those t-shirts out and in the concession stands. Actually, a small, separate kiosk could be a starter kit for you. There's money to be made here and the mark-up is quite substantial. You can co-op with your store on campus or you can go into business for yourself and for your marketing team. Remember, sizes can be a problem as well as storage and your inventory security.

33. Everywhere you go – take a large supply of your business cards. Make them attractive and use front for name, title, school, mailing address, phone, fax, e-mail, etc. – and the back to SELL — SELL — SELL and use that LOGO.

...and get that business card from everyone you meet and shake hands.

34. With your student interns, you are teaching ATTITUDE and WORK ETHIC and getting along with each other.

High tech advances will surprise us more and more everyday in the future. It will be difficult to stay up with all the new and improved resources we'll have at our disposal. This is another reason to network and stay in touch with others in the field so you can share new ideas. A network that you set up that goes across the country and includes the colleges and the pros would seem to be one method of staying up to date. In addition, the marketing publications for sports keep you posted with the latest also.

NOTES

A MESSAGE FROM BILL FOSTER

Bill Foster
P.O. Box 5295
Galveston, Texas 77554
Phone: (409) 737-9470
Fax: (409) 737-4856

ROUTING REMINDER
☐ Principal
☐ Athletic Director
☐ Varsity Club
☐ Booster Club
☐ Football Coach
☐ Basketball Coach
☐ Women's Basketball
☐ Band Director
THIS WORKS FOR ALL

Instead of sending a large brochure or flyer on this brand new book entitled: "HOW TO EARN DOLLARS ($$$$) FOR YOUR TEAM/ORGANIZATION/CLUB BY DIRECT MAIL"......please take a minute to read on......

GOOD NEWS/BAD NEWS......but first the bad news; just about every team/organization/club has money problems -- usually not enough.

NOW FOR THE GOOD NEWS: This book is written, in detail, on how we earned about $40,000 per year with our Fast Break Club at Northwestern University for men's basketball -- all by DIRECT MAIL.

AND it was fun and it'll work for you. This book carefully explains, step by step, how and why it was done. Here's a true story -- and an excellent opportunity for YOU to do the same, depending on how much you need to raise -- big schools -- small schools -- universities, colleges, churches, and yes, it can be done in junior high.

This book should be in every school's library -- it's a "yellow highlighter" special. Most schools/churches, if not all, pay for these books, or it's an investment in your group's future. The GREATEST RETURN ON YOUR INVESTMENT you'll ever make. THIS REALLY WORKS.

ORDER NOW -- only $9.95 plus shipping and handling -- while we're in our first printing. It will be going-going-GONE!

Included is a chapter on how you can STAFF this fundraiser with a very limited budget.

$ How to Earn Dollars $$$
for your
Team / Organization / Club
By
DIRECT MAIL
By Bill Foster

EVERY DETAIL FROM 'A TO Z'

Order NOW by detaching and sending to:

Bill Foster
P.O. Box 5295
Galveston, Texas 77554

Name: _____

Title: _____

School: _____

Mail Address: _____

City: _____ State: _____ Zip Code: _____

Please Send Me: ____ copy(s) of "HOW TO EARN DOLLARS ($$$$) FOR YOUR TEAM/ORGANIZATION/CLUB BY DIRECT MAIL".

(Bus. ID #211207098)

No. of Copies: _____ x $9.95 = _____
Postage/Handling (each) x $1.75 = _____

TOTAL AMOUNT ENCLOSED: $_____

Order Now While They Last!

"*Upward Mobility* is the definitive work today on getting started in coaching and advancing in the profession."
- Rick Majerus

Bill Foster's UPWARD MOBILITY
In Coaching Basketball

Topics Include:

☐ **Professional Advancement: Moving Up the Coaching Ladder**

☐ **Making Your Own Job Better**

☐ **Selecting, Developing and Managing a Quality and Productive Staff**

"There has never been anything definitive written about moving up the job ladder in the coaching profession - - finally, it's here. Upward Mobility is a must read for anyone involved or interested in the profession."
- Chuck Daly

"This manual should be required reading for anyone in the profession or anyone looking at the profession. It is a recipe book for building a successful career. Essential reading. I've ordered copies for my entire staff.... A great gift idea."
- George Raveling

ED. NOTE: ACTUALLY GREAT FOR COACHING ANY SPORT**

ORDER FORM

Please detach and send your completed form to:

Bill Foster
P.O. Box 5295
Galveston, Texas 77554

Name _____

School _____

Address _____

City _____ State _____ Zip _____

Please send me ____ copy(s) of
UPWARD MOBILITY IN COACHING BASKETBAL

Number of Copies ____ x 9.95 ____
Postage & Handling ____ x 1.50 ____

TOTAL ____

(Bus. ID#211207098)

250   *Please allow ten days for delivery. Please make checks payable to Bill Foster.*